CCM IS NOT
THE PROBLEM

IT IS ONLY
A SYMPTOM

ROCK
ON

YOU ARE INVITED

By David C. Bennett, D.Min.

Published by

THE BIBLE FOR TODAY PRESS
900 Park Avenue
Collingswood, New Jersey 08108
U.S.A.
Pastor D. A. Waite, Th.D., Ph.D.
Bible For Today Baptist Church
Church Phone: 856-854-4747
BFT Phone: 856-854-4452
Orders: 1-800-John 10:9
e-mail: BFT@BibleForToday.org
Website: www.BibleForToday.org
fax: 856-854-2464

We Use and Defend
The King James Bible

April, 2013
BFT 4052

ISBN #978-1-56848-084-8

Table of Contents

Publisher's Data.................................... i

Table of Contents.................................. ii

Preface.. iii

Foreword.. iv

Acknowledgments. v

I.   A Warning.................................... 1

II. CCM and the Churches. 11

III. The Musicians of CCM And Where They Lead. 23

IV Does It Matter? 37

Index of Words and Phrases..................... 51

About the Book and Author..................... 68

Preface

This book is not written with animosity toward any church, individual or group. It is not written by an expert musician but it is written by a Baptist preacher with an aching heart and the desire that this small book will be read by many and that their eyes and hearts will be open to what is taking place with what is known as Contemporary Christian Music (CCM). A little research of the footnotes will be a great help to the pastor or any Christian who is concerned with what CCM is doing to the churches.

My prayer is, Lord, "open the eyes of these men, that they may see" the dangers that lie ahead when a church follows the CCM crowd. Pastor, remember you will be held responsible to the Lord for where you lead the Lord's church.

To God be the Glory,
David C. Bennett, D. Min.
Dubbo, NSW, Australia

Foreword

- **The Need**. This little booklet points out the growing acceptance of Contemporary Christian Music (CCM) in churches that were formerly fundamental and separatist. This CCM has brought with it the lowering of standards in these churches that have begun to use it. Dr. Bennett has given many facts to enable the readers to try to keep CCM completely out of their churches.
- **The Author**. Dr. David Bennett is the author of this book. He has been one of the missionaries of the Bible For Today Baptist Church for many years. Our church is his "sending church." Since 1979, He and his wife, Pam, have been faithfully serving the Lord Jesus Christ in the land of Australia. He has two churches and a radio ministry there. He is also one of our faithful Executive Committee members of the Dean Burgon Society (DBS).
- **The Book's Format**. I have taken Dr. Bennett's book and put it into a format that could be used for the printing of the book. Though this has taken some time and patience, it was necessary to be done before it could be sent to the publishers.
- **The Book's Usefulness**. It is our hope and prayer that this book might be used of the Lord to convince and encourage even further those who are concerned about music in their churches. It will equip the reader with important facts to enable them to warn others of the CCM dangers before this music completely transforms their church for the worse.
- **The Readers**. It is hoped that those who receive and read this book might encourage many others to get the book, read it, and urge others to read it as well.

Yours For God's Words,

D. A. Waite

Pastor D. A. Waite, Th.D., Ph.D.

Bible For Today Baptist Church

Acknowledgments

The Bible For Today Baptist Church wishes to thank and to acknowledge the assistance of the following people:

- **The Congregation** of the Bible For Today Baptist Church who received copies of the book and paid for its publication.

- **Yvonne Sanborn Waite**--Pastor Waite's wife, who read the manuscript, and gave helpful suggestions and comments.

- **Tamara Waite**–Pastor Waite's daughter-in-law, who also proofread the book. She offered some useful information that we used in the production of this book.

- **Anne Marie Noyle**--a faithful church supporter and Internet attender from Canada who proofread the book and gave many useful suggestions both for improvement and clarification.

CHAPTER I
A Warning!

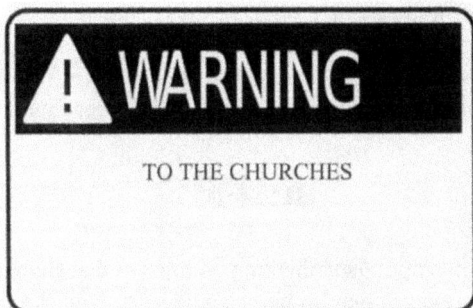

⚠ WARNING

TO THE CHURCHES

ONE STEP AWAY

In Acts 20:29-31 the Apostle Paul told the Ephesian elders *"For I know this, that after my departing shall grievous wolves enter in among you, not sparing the flock. Also of your own selves shall men arise, speaking perverse things, to draw away disciples after them. Therefore watch, and remember, that by the space of three years **I ceased not to warn** every one night and day with tears."*

For three years Paul warned this church in Ephesus of the coming day in which these two types of men would appear in the church. One would come from **WITHOUT** and the other from **WITHIN**!

It has been said that a local church is only one pastor away from liberalism. That might be changed to this; a local church is only one pastor away from new-evangelicalism **and then** taking the next step into liberalism and then into apostasy.

The Apostle also wrote the members of this church to *"Put on the whole armour of God, that ye may be able to stand against the wiles of the devil."* (See Ephesians 6:11.) So here is a local church that has three enemies to be watchful of: (1) men from **WITHOUT;** (2) men from **WITHIN;** and (3) the **WILES** (methods) of the Devil.

THE WILES OF THE DEVIL

Those men from **WITHOUT** and those from **WITHIN** will be used of the Devil to implement the Devil's **WILES,** tricks, and methods. All of this is the Devil's plan to hopefully thwart the work of God in the hearts of men. What is that **one method** the Devil is using today via these men from **WITHOUT** and from **WITHIN** to bring together doctrinally divergent churches?

MUSIC

I suppose it is optimistic thinking on my part that anyone who already is into the contemporary church music would even take the time to read this paper. BUT who knows? As one writer who serves with a Christian para-church organization into the CCM said:

> *"One of the seemingly never-ending controversies surrounding church music is the **volume** which it is played."*

LET IT BE SAID, THE "VOLUME" IS NOT THE ONLY PROBLEM THE CHURCHES HAVE, BUT ALSO THE TYPE OF MUSIC PLAYED! So I ask: *"Does it matter?"* And the answer to that is: *"Yes, it does matter!!!"*

In Ephesians 5:19 the Apostle says *"Speaking to yourselves in psalms and hymns and spiritual songs, **singing and making melody** in your heart to the Lord."* Here, just before Paul speaks to them about these workers of the Devil, he speaks to them about their singing, their music.

MUSIC is ONE *wile*, method, or trick which the Devil is using today to obliterate the doctrinal differences between denominations and bring about an ecumenism through music. Search the Internet and it soon becomes evident that the music used in the Baptist churches is the same used in the Methodist or Presbyterian churches.

This writer admits he is not an expert on music, but did take one or two courses in college in the very early 70's concerning church music. The college had various music lecturers, but the one whose notes I kept the most of were Mr. Charles Bergerson, 1918-2000. Mr. Bergerson was a graduate of Moody Bible Institute and it was while he was a student at Moody that he auditioned and received the position as pianist for the Chicago Symphony. He also sang in a quartet with George Beverly Shea while at Moody. Mr. Bergerson's studies then led him to Grace Theological Seminary in Winona Lake, Indiana, where he earned his masters degree.

I may not be an expert, but Mr. Bergerson certainly comes close to being an expert, so we will be quoting extensive passages from his notes. One set of notes that I have from Mr. Burgerson dates from the year 1972. Now, it must be said up front, that Mr. Bergerson was very, very conservative in his music. That isn't because he was just an old fogey and not in touch with the real world. Please be patient, and read what Mr. Bergerson sought to instill in young preachers, assistant pastors, future school teachers, future music teachers, etc.

SACRED MUSIC

Mr. Bergerson's notes for Unit 1 Introduction to Music--Sacred Music said:

> "*The Bible speaks of 'psalms, hymns, and spiritual songs' in defining sacred music. This is the music used specifically for Biblical worship, praise and service of God. The psalms are hymns of praise and worship, sung to God-- Father, Son, and Holy Spirit,--for His praise and for the edification of believers. Romans 15:9 declares: '. . . sing praise unto Thy name . . .' The hymns are generally songs of prayer to God for His will and blessing. Acts 16:25 specifies: '. . . praying, (they) were hymning God . . .' The spiritual songs or odes are testimonials and exhortations in spiritual concerns among believers. Revelation 14:3 portrays the 144,000 persons who 'sung . . . A new song before the throne, . . . The four living creatures, and the elders . . .' Overlapping of these designations there may be, but the general divisions of church music are clear.*"

Mr. Bergerson continues writing that

> "*Church music has changed through the years. However, it*

has changed the least of any form of music. For instance, the 'Hamburg' tune ('4') has come to us from the apostles' day, sung then in a minor mode and probably used by Paul and Silas in the prison (Acts 16:25)."

Moving on into the notes we read:

"It is indeed gratifying to know that God used the church to produce the means or the notation by which music is preserved. . . . The church is properly credited under God, therefore, as given rise to our present repertoire of good music, sacred, and classical. Indeed, 'every good gift and every perfect gift is from above, . . . From the Father of lights...' (James 1:17) including music!"

CLASSICAL MUSIC

"The term, classical, is given to the broad generality of music which is neither sacred nor popular. This broad term refers to much music of the last four or five centuries." Such is the course of classical music, which began in the church as arrangements of hymn-tunes, not unlike our instrumental and vocal arrangements of today."

As time went on, however, the purpose for classical music,--better performability of the church's music--changed, developing

"its own excuse for being,' as the poet would say, by virtue of its beauty and excellence. THUS, IT DIVORCED ITSELF FROM THE CHURCH AND CARRIED ITSELF BY ITS OWN PURPOSEFULNESS (emphasis added), maintaining basically good standards of styling, rather than existing for the benefit of the church's ministry and testimony."

Now, remember it was 1972 when Mr. Bergerson wrote these notes. Has the music in the churches gotten better or worse? Mr. Bergerson wrote:

"As much of today's music manifests itself to be but the musical accompaniment to the events of the end of this age, it behooves the child of God to discern objectively the what, where, how, and why of music, as of all things, and to guard himself from evil. As Paul writes to the Corinthians: 'There are, it may be, so many kinds of voices in the world, and

none of them is without signification. . . . seek that ye may excel to the edifying of the church.' WE MUST DISCERN THE SIGNIFICATION OF WORLDLY MUSICAL VOICES (Emphasis added)."

At the bottom of this page I wrote the note:

"Classical music was downgraded when it departed from worship of God to humanism."

STUDENTS' RESPONSE TO LECTURES ON MUSIC

In February, 1972, Mr. Bergerson gave the students APPRAISALS AND COMMENTS on the papers the students wrote. He wrote:

*"First, most of you, by far, agreed that the trend of music is continually degrading in its styling and its moral or spiritual value. Today's rock and folk styling of music is to be shunned, most of you agreed. Only six of you stated that you thought the new styles of music could be included in the Christian's music appreciation, some of the **six stating that it could be used to attract people toward Christ** (Emphasis added)."*

These students who believed this in 1972, what type of music would they allow in the church today?! Mr. Bergerson states he

"believes that this kind of music ought not to be used or allowed by the Christian."

CHURCH MUSIC: OBSERVATIONS AND SUGGESTIONS

The name of the teacher is not on this paper so it may or may not have been Mr. Burgerson. Only a few of the **observations** will be given here.

"1. Parts of church youth music are being influenced by the popularization of religion, 'Jesus,' and Gospel songs in the world.

2. The trends in music are part of a larger cultural change that is found in art, literature, the theater, and the church.

3. Putting music in contemporary idioms has the same problems as putting the Gospel into the contemporary idioms of art, commercialized publicity, and 'slang' usage.

4. The world is influencing the church, instead of the church, influencing the world.

5. In too many cases, Christians today want just entertainment; and they are getting it.

6. Set goals on the conservative side and be safe.

7. Se are now reaping what we have sown in these areas: too many years of incompetent musicians, sentimental songs, sick congregational singing, hypocritical worship, and emotionalism at the cost of truth." (Emphasis added.)

LUTHER'S MUSIC

Since Luther's music is often brought to this discussion, it was interesting that one of the papers in my music file form college contained an article from *Christianity Today* written by Harold M. Best, director of the Conservatory of Music at Wheaton College. Mr. Best wrote:

"A misuse of history has overemphasized borrowing. A case in point is Luther's comment (when he was criticized for borrowing a drinking song) that the Devil should not have all the good tunes. But Luther's position must be seen in the fuller context of his convictions about music. Borrowing to him was only a small part of a rich means of expression. When he borrowed, he borrowed excellence only and left mediocrity to the Devil. A skilled musician and a composer, he looked with the greatest admiration to the best music of his time, that of the composer Josquin des Prez. If Luther's total position were injected into the contemporary discussion of church music, it would make him very unpopular."

NOTE THE WORD **"UNPOPULAR"**!!

CHURCH MUSIC TODAY

In Ephesians 5:19 God's Words say:

"Speaking to yourselves in psalms and hymns and spiritual songs, singing and making melody in your heart to the Lord."

Spurgeon, commenting on this verse, said:

> "*Men filled with wine call for a song, and when believers are exhilarated by the divine Spirit they also should have their singing, but they must choose the songs of Zion, such as the Lord himself will account to be true melody.*"

TODAY'S SECULAR MUSIC?

In the *Sydney Daily Telegraph* for the 5th of February, 2013, in the article "HOW A TEEN'S IPOD CAN TELL YOU IF THEY WILL BE IN TROUBLE," a young man is quoted as saying:

> "*The person you are reflects what kind of music you listen to, not the other way around.*"

Interesting! Is this also true of those within the churches using CCM?

WHAT IS THE GOAL OF CCM?

Harold Ockenga is the person responsible for coining the term, "New-Evangelical." In the foreword of Harold Lindsell's book, *THE BATTLE FOR THE BIBLE,* Harold Ockenga wrote:

> "*Neo-evangelicalism was born in 1948 in connection with a convocation address which I gave in the Civic Auditorium in Pasadena. While reaffirming the theological view of fundamentalism, this address repudiated its ecclesiology and its social theory. The ringing call for **a repudiation of separatism** and the summons to social involvement received a hearty response from many Evangelicals. . . . It differed from fundamentalism in its **repudiation of separatism** and its determination to engage itself in the theological dialogue of the day. It had a new emphasis upon the application of the gospel to the sociological, political, and economic areas of life* (Emphasis added)."[1]

So New-Evangelicalism as stated by Ockenga is, the "*repudiation of separatism.*" One method used of the Devil in this "*repudiation*" is **MUSIC**. Is the "*repudiation of separatism*" the goal of CCM? Whether this is or not, will be shown later.

---

[1] http://www.theopedia.com/Harold_Ockenga

THE APOSTLE'S WARNING
TO THE CHURCHES

Now let us go back to Acts 20:29-31 where we read the Apostle Paul speaking to the Ephesian elders saying:

> "*For I know this, that after my departing shall* **grievous wolves enter in** *among you, not sparing the flock. 30 Also of* **your own selves shall men arise**, *speaking perverse things, to draw away disciples after them. 31 Therefore watch, and remember, that by the space of three years I ceased not to warn every one night and day with tears.*"

So, for three years, Paul warned this church with tears concerning the coming day in which this would occur from **without** and from **within**!

Now, **IT MUST** be remembered that, since its birth, there has never been the perfect local church, or the perfect pastor, apart from the Great Shepherd Himself. We cannot go back in time to actually see and hear what it was like to attend a meeting in the Jerusalem church, or the church at Ephesus, for example. However, what we can do, is to read what God has left us in His Words concerning the local church.

In Acts 20:29-31, we learn at least **two things**. Firstly, after Paul's departing, grievous wolves would enter into the local church from **outside**, not sparing the flock of God. Nature tells us the wolf doesn't love the sheep! The wolf sees the sheep as only one thing, and that is to gratify the wolf's pleasure. That word "*grievous*" is also translated "*weighty*" and "*heavy*" elsewhere. These wolves were such that the local church members could not resist their deceptive teachings and tactics. These wolves may have been traveling

teachers, preachers, or evangelists, or an elder called from without by the church.

Secondly, Paul knew that some from **within** the local church itself would teach perverted doctrines to draw disciples unto himself. That word, "*perverse*," has to do with distorting, corrupting, and turning away from something. All of this is to draw the flock from the truth to become the disciples of these wolves!

WARNING FOR TODAY?

Paul warned the church at Ephesus about two types of men that the church had to be aware of, those from without, and those from within. Neither one had the best interests of the local flock in mind. Today these two types of men are leading churches from various denominations together. One of those methods used is MUSIC! **MUSIC is being greatly used to break down the wall of ecclesiastical separation!**

Let it be understood that it is not the purpose in this paper to define what is a New Testament Church, or to teach the Biblical principles of music, but simply to give forth a **warning** to those churches that will LISTEN and to those who have not yet gone the way of CCM.

CHAPTER II
CCM And The
Churches

Just look around at the church scene today, whether it be independent Baptist, Southern Baptist, Methodist, Presbyterian, etc. and you will find **the one thing** they all seem to have in common is the **music**; and with the music is the "*repudiation of separatism*"! A search on the Internet will quickly show the state of the churches in this regard. Chapter Two will look at church groups, several churches, and their music.

INDEPENDENT, SOUTHERN BAPTISTS, GARBC, BBFI & CCM

Personally, I do not believe there is much difference in today's world between the so-called independents (BBFI, GARBC, etc) and Southern Baptists! Permit a digression here. It is because of this lack of **real** difference that it is so hard to imagine why the independents, GARBC, and BBFI spend so much time and money having so called faith missionaries run all over the USA seeking support from churches that are not really any different from the Southern Baptist churches--doctrinally, musically, and denominationally!

SBC, FIRST BAPTIST, DALLAS TX[2 3]

First Baptist Church of Dallas has been led by such well known men as George Truett and W. A. Criswell. Even though the present pastor has been outspoken

---

[2]http://www.firstdallas.org/ministries/music-worship/contemporary-worship/

[3]http://www.firstdallas.org/worship/

on several conservative subjects including gays, the music at First Baptist is CCM.

This is typical CCM staging with the lighting, screens, and sound.

NORTH POINT COMMUNITY CHURCH, ALPHARETTA, GEORGIA (SBC)

This church is pastored by Andy Stanley and is into CCM, as most mega churches are. The web page in the footnote is several years old, but it makes the point where the church is on music[4].

---

[4]http://insidenorthpoint.org/media/2009/12/17/north-point-live-awake-5-free/

Typical CCM staging with all the lighting, screen, raised hands and loud sounds.

THE GENERAL ASSOCIATION OF REGULAR BAPTISTS (GARBC) & CCM

I was reared and saved in a GARB church. I obtained my undergraduate degree from an approved school of the GARBC when they still had the approval system. I was saved, baptized, ordained, and sent to the mission field from churches in fellowship with the GARBC. I had some deep, deep roots in the GARBC, and still have some friends in the GARBC. Therefore, this is written with concern about how some of the churches within the GARBC are deep into this CCM movement. This didn't happen overnight. In fact, the *Baptist Bulletin* (the official organ of the GARBC) reveals just how much of a hold the CCM has on all too many of the GARBC churches.

Sadly, this move away from its once conservative and Biblical position on separation and music has been going on for several years now, as seen in the following article.

Top 50 Worship Songs Used in GARBC Churches

October 15, 2012

"In Christ Alone" by **Keith Getty, Stuart Townsend** (2001)

"Mighty to Save" by Ben Fielding, Reuben Morgan (2006)

"Blessed Be Your Name" by Beth Redman, **Matt Redman** (2002)

"Everlasting God" by **Brenton Brown**, Ken Riley (2005)

"Glorious Day (Living He Loved Me)" by J. Wilbur Chapman, Mark Hall, et al. (2009)

"Forever Reign" by Jason Ingram, Reuben Morgan (2009)

"Your Grace Is Enough" by Matt Maher (2003)

"Revelation Song" by Jennie Lee Riddle (2004)

"Before the Throne of God" by Charlie Lees Bancroft, Vikki Cook (1997)

"How Great Is Our God" by Chris Tomlin, Ed Cash, Jesse Reeves (2004)

"Jesus Messiah" by Chris Tomlin, Daniel Carson, Ed Cash, et al. (2008)

"Amazing Grace (My Chains Are Gone)" by **Chris Tomlin**, John Newton, Louie Giglio (2006)

"Forever" by Chris Tomlin (2001)

"Our God" by Chris Tomlin, Jesse Reeves, Jonas Myrin, et al. (2010)

"Our God Saves" by Brenton Brown, Paul Baloche (2007)

"Christ Is Risen" by Matt Maher, Mia Fiedes (2009)

"Your Name" by Glen Packiam, **Paul Baloche** (2006)

"The Wonderful Cross" by Chris Tomlin, Isaac Watts, et al. (2001)

"Here I Am to Worship" by **Tim Hughes** (2000)

"Wonderful Merciful Savior" by Dawn Rodgers, Eric Wyse (1989)

"You Never Let Go" by Beth Redman, Matt Redman (2005)

"Sing to the King" by Billy Foote, Charles Silvester Horne (2003)

"Counting on God" by Jaren Anderson (2007)

"The Power of the Cross" by Keith Getty, Stuart Townsend (2005)

"Overcome" by Jon Eagan (2007)

"One Way" by Joel Huston (2003)

"You're Worthy of My Praise" by David Ruis (1991)

"Days of Elijah" by Mark Robin (1996)

"You Are God Alone" by Billy Foote (2004)

"You Are My King" by Billy Foote (1996)

"Hosanna (Praise Is Rising)" by Paul Baloche (2005)

"There Is a Redeemer" by Melody Green-Sievright (1982)

"How Deep the Father's Love" by Stuart Townsend (1995)

"Ancient Words" by Lynn DeShazo (2001)

"O Church Arise" by Keith Getty (2005)

"Lord Most High" by Don Harris (1996)

"Fill Me Up" by Don Poythress (2008)

"You Are Holy (Prince of Peace)" by Marc Imboden (1994)
"I Give You My Heart" by Reuben Morgan (1995)
"I Will Rise" by Chris Tomlin (2008)
"All I Have Is Christ" by Jordan Kauflin (2008)
"Take My Life" by Scott Underwood (1995)
"God of Wonders" by Marc Byrd (2000)
"Love the Lord" by Lincoln Brewster (2005)
"Jesus Paid It All" by Alex Nifong (2006)
"My Savior My God" by Aaron Shust (2005)
"Stronger" by Ben Fielding (2007)
"You Are My All in All" by Dennis Jernigan (1991)
"Holy Is the Lord" by Chris Tomlin (2003)
"Let the Praises Ring" by Lincoln Brewster (2002)"[5]

I will be discussing in the next chapter those who have been highlighted in the above article. These musicians have been instrumental in the ecumenism so prevalent today!

GARBC, MEMORIAL BAPTIST, COLUMBUS, OHIO

Memorial is not a mega-church but to stay with the times,
   "the music at MBC is a blend of contemporary and traditional selections that minister to the wide variety and cross sections of people God sends us."[6]

The topic of whether drums should or should not be used in church is not under discussion here, but note the drums and screen with the words of the song displayed. Are they wrong, right or are they really needed? Why is either being used? Are they really necessary for God's people to sing with joyful voices unto the Lord?! A former supporting GARBC church in California went this way and, unfortunately, before we parted company, I happened to be in one of the services. I noted that with the praise team, drums, and screen, there was a lot of noise on the platform, but much less singing by the congregation! The sheep were being entertained!

---

[5]http://baptistbulletin.org/?p=24900

[6]http://www.mbconline.org/ministries/music

It isn't any surprise that one of the Christian schools Memorial recommends is Cedarville University[7]. The footnote below leads to a video that shows how Cedarville teaches traditional as well as CCM. At Cedarville,

> *"Studying contemporary worship at a Christian college like Cedarville University will not only prepare you to be a worship leader, it will inspire you to be a greater worshipper of our great God! Our worship degree program features a combination of study in music, theology, worship, and multimedia studies and allows you to concentrate in areas such as electronic media, music, theater, preseminary, and communication. Private lessons are available in voice, guitar, and piano with an emphasis in contemporary music. Practical experience is built into the worship program, so you'll be prepared to enter your chosen field after graduation. Our goal is to guide you through the ever-changing climate of worship while grounding you in the never-changing truth of God's Word."*[8]

As the schools go, so go the churches!

---

[7]https://www.cedarville.edu/Media/Academics/Music -and-Worship.aspx

[8]http://www.cedarville.edu/Academics/Music-and-Worship/W orship.aspx

GARBC, SAYLORVILLE CHURCH, DES MOINES, IOWA

This church has dropped the name Baptist which is common with many churches using CCM. The Saylorville Church website (note this website still uses the name Baptist) says:

> "*Our services have contemporary music and preaching directly from the Bible. Both the music and the message are the same in both Sunday morning services.*"[9] [10]

Of course with the music there is a change in the Bible version for:

> "*Here at Saylorville, we preach from the Bible but you do not need to bring a Bible to attend. We preach from the English Standard Version* (ESV)."[11]

Now all of this is not to say these people do not love the Lord Jesus Christ. Some of these churches are seeing a growth in numbers, numerous "*professions*" of faith, and baptisms. However, it must be NOTED that this move away from (1) using the name Baptist and (2) using CCM is a slippery slope to further ecumenism. Do a little search and it will soon be found that this statement is true.

---

[9]http://www.saylorvillebaptist.com/im-new/

[10]http://www.youtube.com/watch?feature=player_embedded&v=Lt6VC0gxc84

[11]http://www.saylorvillebaptist.com/im-new/

BAPTIST BIBLE FELLOWSHIP INTERNATIONAL (BBFI)

My wife was saved and baptized in a BBF church. The BBF churches were very evangelistic. Soul-winning was a priority. My wife and I thank the Lord for the BBF pastor that God used to preach the sermon at a funeral that brought her to the Lord Jesus Christ. But through the years, as with most of the Baptist groups, many of the BBFI churches have now adopted CCM. It is sad that many of these once great churches have submitted to CCM.

BBFI, FAIR OAKS CHURCH, FAIRFAX, VIRGINIA

Fair Oaks is the former Bethlehem Baptist Church. Even though the BBFI lists this church as a fellowship church,[12] the pastor's blog says Fair Oaks Church is

"... *a non-denominational congregation* ... "[13] and "... *is part of the Willow Creek Association and is a Fellowship Connection affiliated church.*"[14]

So often with CCM comes a change in association. Therefore it is not a surprise that Fair Oaks' music for:

"... *Sunday services feature contemporary music by our praise and worship band, relevant drama, fun programs for children, multimedia experiences and much more.*"[15]
Entertainment?

---

[12]http://www.zetify.com/churches/all/Baptist%20Bible%20Fellowship%20International-Fairfax-VA-Churches

[13]http://www.davidrstokes.com/?page_id=12

[14]Ibid.

[15]http://vimeo.com/fairoakschurch

LOUD ON PURPOSE BAND!

Note the large screen, lighting, hands raised, and the instruments. Typical CCM.

BBFI, CAPITAL CITY BAPTIST, DES MOINES, IOWA

This church also has a worship band and praise team[16] which is typical CCM. The worship band includes ". . . *acoustic or electric guitar, bass, drums, keyboard, saxophone . . . flute*"[17].

The praise team: **The worship band:**

---

[16]http://www.capitolcitychurch.com/content.cfm?id=338

[17]Ibid.

Again CCM's composition with the screens, guitars, raised hands, and hand held microphones.

INDEPENDENT BAPTISTS (NON-AFFILIATED)

These churches claim not to be affiliated with any group such as the BBFI, SBC, or GARBC. However, some of them do fellowship with the Southwide Baptist Fellowship.

INDEPENDENT BAPTIST: TRINITY BAPTIST, JACKSONVILLE, FLORIDA

This church was pastored for many years by Bob Gray whose sermons were printed in the *Sword of the Lord*. Gray spent several years on the mission field after he left Trinity. He died just before he was to stand trial for pedophilia.

Trinity has their Church Life Worship Band. The sound is typical CCM.[18] If you are up, for it you can also listen to some of the songs of this band.[19] Typical CCM!

---

[18]http://www.tbc.org/pages/page.asp?page_id=15258

2

[19]http://graceandpurposemusic.bandcamp.com/album /our-god

CHURCH OF THE HIGHLANDS, CHATTANOOGA, TENNESSEE

This church was once an independent Baptist church which was pastored many years by Dr. Lee Roberson. If this church had any major emphasis when Dr. Roberson was alive, it would have been soul-winning. Sadly, little emphasis was put on separation. Today it is strongly in the SBC and using CCM.

Their website says *"Worship Set for the 9:15 (Classic) Service"* and *"Worship Set for the 10:45 (Contemporary) Service"*[20]. Classic is traditional and contemporary is CCM!

> *"On Saturday nights, if you come by our gym, the **sounds of electric guitars and drums** may buzz your car as you drive down Hunter Road. We allow a lot of **Christian bands** to host concerts at our church on Saturday nights."*[21]

CCM means LOUD and being dressed down.

> *". . . the power of music is undeniable. It seems to tap into deeper and more honest places than words alone ever could. It has been said that music is the language of the soul. We believe it. That's why attending a concert for your favorite band can become a lifetime memory, with thousands of people singing songs that connect with their experiences.*

---

[20]http://thehighlands.cc/blog/posts/what-to-expect-at-church-tomorrow

[21]http://thehighlands.cc/uniqueness

Sundays are like that at The Highlands."[22]

These churches may get the numbers, but CCM is their death.

> "*The Highlands worship team along with Church of the Highlands at large is continually growing and changing in our attempts to provide people with unforgettable encounters with God. We are committed to growing the most effective worship team in order to create a weekend experience you won't soon forget. The Highlands' band consists of acoustic guitar, electric guitar, drums, bass, and keyboards. Our worship choir for our classic service is off-the-hook, and we sing all types of classic songs to the Lord together. On special occasions we will use different instruments to enhance the worship experience.*"[23]

CLOSING THOUGHT

In closing this chapter, the reality is that CCM is much the same in whatever denomination it finds itself. It is usually **LOUD**, **has dressed down performers**, electric and non-electric **guitars**, **electric key boards, raised hands, microphones** being held in the hands CLOSE to the mouth as if it is ready to be eaten, **screens, and lighting**. This is the entertainment of CCM. **CCM is a progressive downward slippery slope into new evangelicalism which will definitely lead into out and out liberalism!**

---

[22]http://thehighlands.cc/worship

[23]Ibid.

CHAPTER III
The Musicians of CCM
And Where They Lead

As I write these words, I am closer to seventy than I am to sixty-five. It still amazes me why some Baptist preachers my age are taking their churches into CCM. I "think" I understand just a "little" why some of the younger preachers might, but NOT those my age or older! THEY DEFINITELY SHOULD KNOW BETTER AND SHOULD BE HELPING THE YOUNGER TO TAKE A STAND AGAINST CCM.

> *"The hoary head is a crown of glory, if it be found in the way of righteousness"* Proverbs 16:31!

Now I know Spurgeon lived in another century and he would be considered an old fuddy duddy in today's CCM churches, but his words still have that ring of truth to them. Here are a few statements he made concerning music and worship in the Lord's churches.

> *"WE do not use instrumental music in the worship of God because we consider that it would be a violation of the simplicity of our worship. We think it far better to hear the voices of Christian men and women than all the sounds which can be made by instruments."*
>
> *"HAD I no conscientious objection to instrumental music in worship, I would still, I think, be compelled to admit that all the instruments that were ever devised by men, however sweetly attuned, are harsh and grating compared with the unparalleled sweetness of the human voice."*
>
> *"ARCHITECTURE, apparel, music, liturgies, these are neither spirit nor life: let those rest on them who will; we can do without them, by God's help."*

A FEW NEW TESTAMENT SCRIPTURES CONCERNING MUSIC:

Since the church is a New Testament organism, it is the New Testament to which we will look concerning music individually and corporately. It is doubtful any of these verses would be a defense for the use of CCM but someone will try, it is certain.

MUSICK:

Luke 15:25 *"Now his elder son was in the field: and as he came and drew nigh to the house, he heard <u>MUSICK</u> and dancing."* **No, this doesn't make dancing in the church ok.**

SINGING:

Ephesians 5:19 *"Speaking to yourselves in psalms and hymns and spiritual songs, <u>singing</u> and making melody in your heart to the Lord"*

Colossians 3:16 *"Let the word of Christ dwell in you richly in all wisdom; teaching and admonishing one another in psalms and hymns and spiritual songs, <u>singing</u> with grace in your hearts to the Lord."*

SING:

Romans 15:9 *"And that the Gentiles might glorify God for his mercy; as it is written, For this cause I will confess to thee among the Gentiles, and <u>sing</u> unto thy name."*

1 Corinthians 14:15 *"What is it then? I will pray with the spirit, and I will pray with the understanding also: I will <u>sing</u> with the spirit, and I will <u>sing</u> with the understanding also."*

Hebrews 2:12 *"Saying, I will declare thy name unto my brethren, in the midst of the church will I <u>sing</u> praise unto thee."*

James 5:13 *"Is any among you afflicted? let him pray. Is any merry? let him <u>sing</u> psalms."*

Revelation 15:3 *"And they <u>sing</u> the song of Moses the servant of God, and the song of the Lamb, saying, Great and marvellous are thy works, Lord God Almighty; just and true are thy ways, thou King of saints."*

SONG:

Revelation 5:9 *"And they sung a new <u>song</u>, saying, Thou art worthy to take the book, and to open the seals thereof: for thou wast slain, and hast redeemed us to God by thy blood out of every kindred, and tongue, and people, and nation"*

Revelation 14:3 *"And they sung as it were a new <u>song</u> before the throne, and before the four beasts, and the elders: and no man could learn that <u>song</u> but the hundred and forty and four thousand, which were redeemed from the earth."*

Revelation 15:3 *"And they sing the <u>song</u> of Moses the servant of God, and the <u>song</u> of the Lamb, saying, Great and marvellous are thy works, Lord God Almighty; just and true are thy ways, thou King of saints."*

SONGS:

Ephesians 5:19 *"Speaking to yourselves in psalms and hymns and spiritual <u>songs</u>, <u>singing</u> and making melody in your heart to the Lord"*

Colossians 3:16 *"Let the word of Christ dwell in you richly in all wisdom; teaching and admonishing one another in* *psalms and hymns and spiritual <u>songs</u>, <u>singing</u> with grace in your hearts to the Lord."*

SUNG:

Mark 14:26 *"And when they had <u>sung</u> an hymn, they went out into the mount of Olives."*

SANG:

Acts 16:25 *"And at midnight Paul and Silas prayed, and <u>sang</u> praises unto God: and the prisoners heard them."*

INSTRUMENTS OF MUSIC IN THE NEW TESTAMENT

TRUMPET:

Matthew 6:2 *"Therefore when thou doest thine alms, do not sound a <u>trumpet</u> before thee, as the hypocrites do in the synagogues and in the streets, that they may have glory of men. Verily I say unto you, They have their reward."*

Matthew 24:31 *"And he shall send his angels with a great sound of a <u>trumpet</u>, and they shall gather together his elect from the four winds, from one end of heaven to the other."*

1 Corinthians 14:8 *"For if the <u>trumpet</u> give an uncertain sound, who shall prepare himself to the battle?"0*

1 Corinthians 15:52 *"In a moment, in the twinkling of an eye, at the last trump: for the <u>trumpet</u> shall sound, and the dead shall be raised incorruptible, and we shall be changed."*

Hebrews 12:19 *"And the sound of a <u>trumpet</u>, and the voice* *of words; which voice they that heard intreated that the word should not be spoken to them any more:"*

Revelation 1:10 *"I was in the Spirit on the Lord's day, and heard behind me a great voice, as of a <u>trumpet</u>,"*

Revelation 4:1 *"After this I looked, and, behold, a door was opened in heaven: and the first voice which I heard was as it were of a <u>trumpet</u> talking with me; which said, Come up hither, and I will shew thee things which must be hereafter."*

Revelation 8:13 *"And I beheld, and heard an angel flying through the midst of heaven, saying with a loud voice, Woe, woe, woe, to the inhabiters of the earth by reason of the other voices of the <u>trumpet</u> of the three angels, which are yet to sound!"*

Revelation 9:14 *"Saying to the sixth angel which had the <u>trumpet</u>, Loose the four angels which are bound in the great river Euphrates."*

HARP:

1 Corinthians 14:7 *"And even things without life giving sound, whether pipe or <u>harp</u>, except they give a distinction in the sounds, how shall it be known what is piped or harped?"*

HARPS:

Revelation 5:8 *"And when he had taken the book, the four beasts and four and twenty elders fell down before the Lamb, having every one of them <u>harps</u>, and golden vials full of odours, which are the prayers of saints."*

Revelation 14:2 *"And I heard a voice from heaven, as the voice of many waters, and as the voice of a great thunder: and I heard the voice of harpers harping with their <u>harps</u>:"*

> **Revelation 15:2** *"And I saw as it were a sea of glass mingled with fire: and them that had gotten the victory over the beast, and over his image, and over his mark, and over the number of his name, stand on the sea of glass, having the <u>harps</u> of God."*

None of these verses when considered in context (or even out of context) would lend itself to what is taking place in the music of churches today. The noise, the gyrations, and all the hype does not seem to be making more spiritual and mature believers either. Someone replies, "it is just your age that makes you not like CCM, or you are being too legalistic." As Spurgeon said:

> *"I cannot suppose that at the last great day our Lord Jesus Christ will say to anyone, 'You were not worldly enough. You were too jealous over your conduct, and did not sufficiently conform to the world.' No, my brethren, such a wrong is impossible. He Who said, 'Be ye perfect, evan as your Father which is in heaven is perfect,' has set before you a standard beyond which you can never go."*

It is hard to imagine the Lord and disciples walking to the Mount of Olives singing with the accompaniment of guitars and drums. Be real! <u>CCM is popular because it is fleshly and worldly</u>! As simple as that.

IN CHAPTER TWO, I highlighted seven musicians in the GARBC's *Baptist Bulletin* article "**Top 50 Worship Songs Used in GARBC Churches**" **October 15, 2012.**[24] There was no WARNING with the article, so in this chapter the spotlight will be directed mainly on these musicians, their doctrinal positions, and affiliations which affect their music, and in turn, will affect your local church.

---

[24]http://baptistbulletin.org/?p=24900

"Church music is changing. Again"[25] [26]

It is important to know with whom these musicians work and fellowship with for that is an indication of where they are theologically. From the research, **none of them have a problem with the charismatic movement or Rome**! As we work our way through these seven, a pattern of ecumenism is clearly seen which will have a detrimental affect on the listeners, their spiritual life, and their churches.

It is natural for many of those who sing the songs written by these musicians such as Getty will go to listen to them when they come to their city to perform. At these performances it will be a multi-denominational gathering.

Egypt in Scripture is a type of the world and CCM is simply going back into Egypt. CCM is simply the fish, the cucumbers, the melons, the leeks, the onions, and the garlic of Egypt (Numbers 11:5)! True believer, that is what you left behind when you came to the Lord Jesus Christ. He has much better in store! However, many of the pastors are leading the sheep back into Egypt, not thinking, or perhaps not caring about the consequences that lie before them. Are these pastors those which Paul speaks of as coming from **WITHIN** and the musicians those from **WITHOUT**?

CCM is the same music the believer left behind in the world. The rhythm and beat are of the world no matter what the words are. If you go to the websites listed in the footnotes, most of the time you cannot really hear the words for the loudness of the instruments. The beat is that of the world. One would not know the difference in most cases if these gatherings were Christian or not. The young people are dressed like the world's young people. The gyrations are of the world and appeal to the flesh. Be assured, CCM follows the world, and not the other way around!   (1 John 2:15)

---

[25] http://baptistbulletin.org/?p=24904

[26] http://baptistbulletin.org/?p=24904

THE SEVEN

In Christ Alone

National Day Conference Uniting Theology & Worship
At Wycliffe Hall, Oxford
Wednesday 17th June 2009, 10am–4.30pm

KEITH GETTY[27]. Keith Getty has no issue with associating with the mixed multitude listed above. This gathering says it is

". . . *celebrating the* **unity and diversity of theology and music across the denominations.**" *THIS IS OUT AND OUT ECUMENISM! IS THIS WHAT THE PASTORS OF THOSE BBFI, GARBC, AND INDEPENDENT BAPTIST CHURCHES DESIRE FOR THE SHEEP? It must be, or otherwise, they would be warning the sheep rather than leading them into CCM! Where are the discerning believers in today's churches? Have the older believers surrendered to the hour? Think about this; DIVERSITY OF THEOLOGY! Theology is comprised of doctrine. So what doctrine are you willing to get soft on, abandon, or not speak about when in*

---

[27]http://www.musicademy.com/2009/05/in-Christ-alo
ne-louie-giglio-tim-hughes-keith-getty-and-others-at-oxford-c
onference/

certain groups? This is the ecumenism that this kind of thinking is taking the churches![28]

STUART TOWNSEND is another of the seven. His associations are similar to the Getty's in that it is very ecumenical.

> *"Stuart continues to be involved in leading worship with a number of organizations, including Spring Harvest, New Frontiers, CARE, Worship Together, and Mandate, and will be at Northern Ireland's New Horizon festival."[29]*

The New Frontiers USA website[30] (ConfluenceUSA) promotes Confluence.

> *"It is essential to recognize God's activity if you want to see charismatic gifts increase."[31] "Confluence is a place where the reformed, the charismatic, and the mission-minded converge to equip and serve the church to transform communities."[32]*

This is a mixed multitude! Is this what the GARBC is in agreement with? Would it not have been beneficial if the *Baptist Bulletin* had written a warning to the churches concerning these musicians in the same October, 2012, issue!? Isn't it still true you are known by the company you keep?

---

[28]http://www.stuarttownend.co.uk/about/gallery/

[29]http://worshiptogether.com/worship-leaders/?iid=2

16440

[30]http://www.newfrontiersusa.org/cms/

[31]Ibid.

[32]http://www.confluenceblog.com/

Here we have noted only two of the seven so far and the ecumenism is so blatant even a soft separatist (if there is such a person) would see it. Do the pastors of these churches really believe this hodgepodge will not have any spiritual affect on his young people?! **Mark my word, this so-called unity of theology and music is the precursor to apostasy! There is "death in the pot" in CCM!**

MATT REDMAN and family now live in the UK but
> *"Previously they were part of Passion City Church in Atlanta, USA with pastors Louie and Shelley Giglio, and continue to work alongside the Passion movement."*[33]

LOUIS GIGLIO is leader of the Passion movement and
> *"PASSION CITY CHURCH - On May 11, 2008, Chris Tomlin announced that he was leaving his church to start a new church in Atlanta with Louie (called Passion City Church). Louie confirmed this rumor on The Passion Podcast on June 27, 2008. Passion City Church held its first service on February 15, 2009, in Atlanta at The Tabernacle. Louie and his wife were members of North Point Community Church in Atlanta for 13 years until the founding of Passion City Church."*[34]

Are you beginning to see how all these CCM musicians run in the same crowd? And that crowd is an ecumenical crowd! **CHRIS TOMLIN** is one of the seven under discussion and he too is associated with Giglio.

BRENTON BROWN attends "Calvary Community church in Thousand Oaks, CA."[35] [36]

---

[33] http://www.mattredman.com/bio

[34] http://www.cbn.com/700club/guests/bios/louiegigli o092409.aspx

[35] http://www.brentonbrown.com/bio.html

[36] http://www.calvarycc.org/contentpages.aspx?parent navigationid=8166&viewcontentpageguid=ec8dd41f-376b-45 72-b0c8-dc4fae03c1bb

Calvary Community is a typical CCM church with the lighting, screens, and I am sure, the noise. Brenton Brown also associates with Worship Together.[37] **Brown's** band is known as **Worship Republic** and their logo is shown below.

I have not a clue what the image depicts unless it is bowing to the image in the book of Daniel when the music was played. **Whatever it is, it is scary!!!!! to say the least. This is CCM!**

WORSHIP REPUBLIC

CHRIS TOMLIN frequents Worship Together as well, so he too is in agreement with the ecumenism found there. As with most, if not all CCM'ers, there is the dressed down scruffy look.

---

[37] http://worshiptogether.com/worship-leaders/?iid=2

16462

Note, the photos are the typical CCM dressed down look, hands raised, and lots of lights! This is CCM along with its LOUDNESS. Forget the suit and tie but explain how this look; T-shirt, beanie, and leather jacket is much if any different from the world's? The raising of the hands in church used to mean either you were from the south, or a Pentecostal, but that is no longer the case! How do those churches, that once were very jealous of doctrine, allow this into their ranks? **Is it the music that will bring in the great falling away?**

PAUL BALOCHE attends and is one of the worship pastors[38] of the non-denominational Community Fellowship in Lindale, Texas, which also has Awana.[39] Awana is another book! Baloche has co-written songs with Matt Redman, Brenton Brown, Tim Hughes, Chris Tomlin, and others. He is by no means a separatist. He has also participated in the Saddleback worship and music conference. At the Saddleback worship and music conference in 2009, Baloche and friends are singing the Beatles' Twist & Shout.[40] It has the dressed down look and the noise, but no lights, as it was filmed during the day. Has it sunk in yet that CCM is a mixed multitude going back into Egypt!?

---

[38]http://ccflindale.org/index.php?option=com_conten t&task=view&id=24&Itemid=41

[39]http://www.ccflindale.org/

[40]http://www.youtube.com/watch?v=T_L74NU9eyk

TIM HUGHES attends Soul Survivor Church,, and also associates with Worship Together.[41]

Tim Hughes is truly an ecumenist.

> *"A night together to celebrate Pentecost - featuring Gary Clarke, Peter Wilson & Joel Houston (Hillsong), Agu Irukwu & Tribe of Judah (Jesus House), and Nicky Gumbel & Tim Hughes (HTB)."*[42]

Celebrating Pentecost with Pentecostals. This is CCM and the independents, GARBC, BBFI, and SBC pastors do not seem to care!!!!

How far will CCM take the churches?
> *"The night will involve inspiring visuals, lighting, dance, and creativity as Tim is joined by a host of amazing musicians from around the globe. **This promises to be an incredible night of worship.**"*[43]

Visuals, lighting, dance, and creativity is worship to these CCM musicians! WHERE WILL THIS ALL END?

---

[41] http://www.worshiptogether.com/worship-leaders/?iid=216453

[42] http://www.worshipcentral.org/blog/worshipcentral/tim-hughes/the-ministry-of-the-spirit

[43] http://www.myspace.com/timhughesmusic/blog

CHAPTER IV
Does It Matter?

CCM is a growing problem among the churches today, BUT CCM is not **THE** PROBLEM! As the title of the book says, **CCM is only a symptom**. When a pastor who is "WITHIN" introduces a church to CCM, which is "WITHOUT," he also has other objectives that have already been or will be implemented.

> Acts 20:29-30 *"For I know this, that after my departing shall grievous wolves **enter in among you** (**WITHOUT--CCM**), not sparing the flock. 30 Also of your own selves (**WITHIN-- PASTORS**) shall men arise, speaking perverse things, to draw away disciples after them."*

What other changes will go out when CCM is allowed in?

FIRST, the name "Baptist" will usually, if not always, be dropped. The SBC, GARBC, BBFI, and Independents have all been greatly infected with CCM and with it has come the dropping of the name Baptist. In the GARBC's *Baptist Bulletin* for February, 2013, the Council of Eighteen wrote

> *"At their November 2011 meeting, the Council of Eighteen approved a new policy stating that a GARBC church 'must publicly identify itself as a Baptist church in its corporate documents and in its practice.' In essence, the new policy allows churches to remain in fellowship with the GARBC even if Baptist is not in their published name. The policy retains our historic emphasis on the way a church functions. These churches will continue to be identified parenthetically as 'a Baptist church' in our GARBC directory"* (Emphasis

added).[44]

Now the excuse for this is because, in the formation of the GARBC, the constitution ". . . *never specified exactly how a Baptist church should be named*."[45]

Really now, would those who were instrumental in the formation of the GARBC have EVER IMAGINED it would be necessary to state only churches who openly identified themselves as a **BAPTIST** church would EVEN DESIRE to be associated with the GARBC?! The reasoning of the GARBC Council of Eighteen sounds like a group of men that have capitulated to the trends of the day in which they live.

SECONDLY, the King James Bible will be removed and replaced with one of the new versions and in the Baptist circle it is usually the NASV or ESV. To the CCM crowd, the King James Bible is archaic and too hard to understand. One will not find any of the churches mentioned in this book that continue to use the King James Bible. Now, this is not to say that every church that uses the King James Bible is what God would have them to be, but it is saying many churches that go down the road of CCM, will eventually drop the use of the King James Bible.

THIRDLY, the ecclesiastical separatism of days past is too strict and harsh. One GARBC pastor in a sermon entitled Reformed Theology (Part Two)[46] quotes Roland Hill (1744-1833):

> "*I do not want the walls of separation between different orders of Christians to be destroyed, but only lowered, that we may shake hands a little easier over them.*"[47]

It isn't surprising then that this GARBC pastor approves of Hill's statement, for in 1995 a similar statement was made by the then newly elected

---

[44]http://baptistbulletin.org/?p=27236

[45]Ibid.

[46]http://www.saylorvillechurch.com/index.php?s=reformed+theology

[47]http://en.wikiquote.org/wiki/Denominationalism

GARBC National Representative.

> *"CHRISTEN IS GARBC'S NEW CHIEF—Soon after Dr. Paul Tassell stepped down last year as National Representative of the General Association of Regular Baptist Churches, he gave Search Committee Chairman Bill Rudd a long list of reasons why he felt Dr. Richard Christen should succeed him at this post. At its annual meeting in Toledo last month, with Dr. Warren Wiersbe the main speaker (see 4/15, 6/1 CCs), indeed Christen was elected by a 75.2 percent vote to be the new National Rep. A two-thirds majority was required. Dr. Mark Jackson has served as interim National Representative and will stay during the transition. Three new churches were added to the GARBC and 17 exited, leaving the total at 1,458 churches. In a recent 'Vision Statement,' Christen said 'We must allow for differences in drawing the lines of secondary separation . . . We must shape a positive outlook and image . . .' Prior to his election, he told the gathering: 'Instead of a two-foot thick wall around our GARBC, let's build a sturdy picket fence around us.' This is amazing, but sad! Just how much protection and safety does a picket fence provide? Nehemiah built a WALL! Sadly, we see no signs that the GARBC will reverse its present downward course."*[48]

Brother Huffman was correct, for many pickets have been removed from that fence of which Christen spoke in 1995.

Sadly, even before Christen came on the scene, Dr. Paul Tassell had gone very soft on ecclesiastical separation. Now I use the word *"sadly"* because Paul Tassell was our sending church pastor when we first came to Australia in 1979. Here is a little history.

> *"GARBC was formed as a fundamentalist, and strictly separatist, entity--a GARBC historian has stated that GARBC was founded 'to provide a militant, missionary-minded, Biblically separated haven of Fundamentalism.' Therefore, were there not a willingness and desire to obey God in the matter of Biblical separation, there would have been neither*

48

reason nor justification for the existence of GARBC. In fact, in the Doctrinal Statement of the GARBC, as well as in a number of its 'official' Literature Items (specifically Item Numbers One, Two, Six, Ten, Twelve, and Thirteen), its long-standing historical position on separation is clear and thoroughly Biblical. [Nevertheless, at GARBC's 1987 Annual Meeting in Anaheim, almost like a Ripley's Believe It or Not, the GARBC's ruling Council of Eighteen rejected (by a 2-1 margin) a motion to formalize its own 15 different Literature Items as the 'official position' of the GARBC. The Council even refused to recognize the Literature Items as "accurate commentaries" of the GARBC! **All the outspoken separatists were also defeated for the Council in the election that year**.] *GARBC continues to state a 'belief' that it will not follow in practice (2/03, GARBC official Internet website)-- 'The GARBC separates from theological liberalism and compromising accommodation.'*

Dr. Paul N. Tassell has been highly respected in GARBC. In 1979, Tassell was selected to be the new National Representative; he came with an image of a tough-minded supporter of secondary separation. *When he spoke at a GARBC Conference in Dayton, Ohio, he said that there are fundamentalists today who shy away from the* separatist position of the GARBC. *He called them "expedient fundamentalists" because they do not want to get involved in the fight for faith. He went on to criticize them as irresponsible fundamentalists who would invite whomever they wished to their pulpits, even the pope:*

'What you do as a pastor, what you do as a college president, what you do as a missionary agency executive, does indeed matter to the whole fundamentalist cause. Who you invite to speak on your platform says volumes about the seriousness of your dedication to Biblical separation. We must be fundamentalists who realize our responsibility to the whole cause of Scriptural separation from apostasy and compromising evangelicals. It's a matter of Biblical integrity. Let's be obedient fundamentalists.'

In 1983, Tassell even authored a book, Pathways to Power, where he states on page 57: 'We must remain true to [the GARBC] separatist position. We must clearly understand and determine to uphold that sacred scriptural purpose.'

Yet while serving as GARBC's National Representative, this same man defended Cedarville College (where he was a trustee) when it invited compromising speakers and has a godless psychology curriculum rivaling that of secular colleges! Even more incredible, at the 1986 GARBC Conference in Grand Rapids, Michigan, Dr. Tassell became the first National Representative in GARBC history to rebuke GARBC churches for too much separation! He pled for less separation less separation and for Regular Baptists to cease criticizing other movements and organizations. He said that organizations like Moody Bible Institute and Word of Life should be appreciated more and not criticized. He said he sees the purpose for the existence of the GARBC as primarily 'fellowship and ministry.' While he wanted the GARBC to be separated from apostasy and infidelity, **he no longer warned against neo-evangelicalism**. This is the precise area of his and the GARBC's change. Neither any longer think of Biblical separation as including separation from disobedient brethren (cf. Rom. 16:17; Titus 3:10; 2 Thes. 3:6,14,15; 2 Jn. 10,11). Moreover, their position has so shifted on Biblical separation that the GARBC is now separating from those who criticize their compromises.

Tassell officially stated his new anti-separatist position at a 6/25/90 private meeting, just prior to the Niagara Falls Conference, when a group of pastors requested a position clarification meeting with the Council of Eighteen. Tassell publicly stated before the whole group (approximately 100 pastors) that he had changed his position. He admitted that in 1985 he came to the conclusion that he was tired of 'scrubbing for surgery' (using Dr. Paul R. Jackson's analogy that likened ecclesiastical separation to a surgeon's sterilization of his instruments and hands before surgery). He had changed his views on separation! **He no longer wanted to practice separation**. Rather, he wanted to 'get to the surgery,' which is the preaching of the Gospel. Biblical separation got in the way. It limited and troubled him. He discounted the fact that the success of 'surgery' depends on the 'scrubbing. (Adapted in part from What Happened to the GARBC at Niagara Falls?, pp. 18-19 & 22-25.) [Tassell resigned as National Representative in late1994 due, to health reasons;] his successor, Dr. Richard Christen, a *non-separatist, resigned in 7/95, after only one month in office, because he 'didn't have peace about it.' The current National Rep is John Greening."*[49]

Today under the leadership of John Greening, when a church requests the GARBC home office for assistance in finding a pastor, some of the questions the church is required to answer under *"church preferences"*[50] are: (1) Bible versions (2) dress styles for services and (3) Worship style. In Worship style a church may pick from four; (1) Blended (2) Contemporary (3) Hymns/Praise Choruses and (4) Traditional. A preacher seeking a GARBC church through the home office must fill out the Candidate form[51] which asks (1) Bible version (2) Worship style and (3) Mission agencies you recommend. From the questions asked on these two forms a separatist would find it hard to make the GARBC home.

Before leaving this, it must be mentioned that this writer knows personally a few GARBC pastors who have not succumbed to CCM, but they are of the more elderly men. However, as is seen from Paul Tassell, even the grey haired man may jump the ship of ecclesiastical separation. It would seem to this writer that most of the younger men associating with the GARBC have sold out to CCM and all that goes with it.

Back to the GARBC pastor and his sermon mentioned earlier, very early into this same sermon, he mentions four Reformed men. This pastor's people not only enjoy listening to these Reformed men, but he also **encourages them to listen to them**. He calls them the "rock stars" of Reformed theology. These men are, John Piper, Mark Driscoll, Tim Keller, and Matt Chandler. Most, if not all of these men, are associated with Together for the Gospel[52] or The Gospel Coalition.[53] These two groups are composed primarily of what is known as the

---

[49]http://www.rapidnet.com/~jbeard/bdm/Psychology/garbc/inclu.htm

[50]http://www.garbc.org/?page_id=9120

[51]http://www.garbc.org/?page_id=8920

[52]http://t4g.org/

[53]http://thegospelcoalition.org/

new-Calvinists[54] which incorporates Calvin's theology, a very weak stance on ecclesiastical separation, and the trappings of CCM.

"Together 4 the Gospel" is certainly one of the organizations that fits Rowland Hill's statement.
> *"Together for the Gospel began as a friendship between four pastors. These friends differed on issues such as baptism and the charismatic gifts. But they were committed to standing together for the main thing—the gospel of Jesus Christ."*[55]

See how low the wall is here (if there is a wall) or how many of the pickets are missing from the fence? People can be personal friends but these organizational gatherings are more than just individual friendship. This has evolved into a gathering that involves many churches and denominations.

These Baptists accepting CCM have repudiated almost everything those who have gone before held dear. The **King James Bible** was the Bible preached from most, if not all, the SBC, GARBC, BBFI, and independent Baptist churches before 1970. The last three groups were not soft and weak on ecclesiastical separation and all four groups were not ashamed of the name Baptist before this contemporary movement gained momentum!

In reality, does it really matter whether CCM is used or not? As stated earlier, there are at least three areas (the King James Bible, ecclesiastical separation, and the Baptist name) that are relinquished with the adoption of CCM. Many, if not most, of these pastors and churches go down this road to draw the numbers (professions) and isn't that what it's all about? Does obtaining the all important numbers require using CCM and forsaking the name Baptist, the King James Bible and separation? (1 John 2:15; Romans 12:2)

If a church claims to be Baptist, why not declare such for all to see?[56] The name Baptist is not a name to be ashamed of, or to shun, just because there are

---

[54]http://www.metropolitantabernacle.org/Sword-And -Trowel/Sword-and-Trowel-Articles/The-Merger-of-Calvinis m-with-Worldliness

[55]http://t4g.org/about/

[56]http://www.saylorvillechurch.com/im-new/

some going under the name that shouldn't be. Let it be understood that Baptistic and Baptist are not the same!

The issue on the English Bible is not only about the King James Bible, but the Greek text underlying the King James. All the new versions use the Critical Greek text developed in the 1800's by Westcott and Hort in their opposition to the Textus Receptus.

> "*At the age of 23, in late 1851, Hort wrote to a friend: 'I had no idea till the last few weeks of the importance of texts, having read so little Greek Testament, and dragged on with* **the villainous Textus Receptus**. . . . *Think of that vile Textus Receptus leaning entirely on late MSS.; it is a blessing there are such early ones.'*"[57]

The Greek text of the King James Bible is supported by the majority of the manuscript evidence. These manuscripts may not be as old as those few underlying the new versions, but that is due to the fact that the majority of the manuscripts are based on manuscripts that were worn out through use in the churches. The manuscripts underlying the new versions were not used by the churches, but were hidden away in Egypt.[58] The versions based on the Critical Greek text omit in total the number of words contained in 1 and 2 Peter. How can anyone say there is no doctrine affected by these omissions?

Actually, there are over 8,000 differences in the Gnostic Critical Greek New Testament Text and the Received Greek New Testament Text that underlies the King James Bible. In those 8,000 differences, there are over 356 doctrinal passages that are involved. See Dr. Jack Moorman's book on *8,000 Differences Between The Critical Text and The Textus Receptus* (BFT #3084 @ $20.00 + S&H).

The CCM churches are weak--**very weak**--on ecclesiastical separation. This is the **PROBLEM** from which CCM and the other objectives take root. Since this writer has had considerable affiliation with both the GARBC and the BBFI, it is with a great sadness to view the departure of these two groups from

---

[57]http://www.revisedstandardversion.net/text/wnp/id_3.html#_ftnref3

[58]http://biblefortoday.org/bennett/Articles/tentative.htm

the positions they once held. Whether those positions were in print or not, they were in practice.

The GARBC's John Greening said
> "*There are other independent Baptists who share our convictions. I want to make new friends with them*"[59].

This is the thinking of organizations, but should it be the thinking of a local church? Where does this type of thought take a church? Greening went on to say:
> "*The GARBC is not a closed club. The speakers we have had at our conference last year, this year, and will have next year, are indicative of that.*"

The proof of that is Tim Jordan, pastor of Calvary Baptist Church and Chancellor at Calvary Baptist Seminary, Lansdale, PA. Jordan was a speaker at the 2010 GARBC conference and is typical of the second generation who is moving or has moved away from the separatist position.
> "*Jordan made it clear that he is all for the recent change of mood among Baptists, calling it an enormous Duh.*"[60]

Jordan also addressed such things as
> "*. . . dress codes, the organ music, the war over Bible translations*" and "*making a clear distinction between the baggage of cultural fundamentalism and the ideas of historic fundamentalism.*"[61]

With Jordan saying what he said at the GARBC conference in 2010, it comes as no surprise that at the Calvary Baptist Seminary's 2011 "Advancing the Church Conference," the keynote speaker was Southern Baptist Mark Dever.[62] Mark Dever is a
> "*five point Calvinist, Credo-Baptist, Covenant Theology,*"

---

[59]http://baptistbulletin.org/?p=9427

[60]Ibid.

[61]Ibid.

[62]http://www.cbs.edu/atc-conference/speakers.html

Amillennial."[63]

Be assured most seminarians are impressionable. Is this one of the seminaries the GARBC is now promoting? Undoubtedly it is!

Calvary Seminary's 2013 keynote speaker is D. A. Carson.[64] Carson is an advocate of the Critical Greek text and research professor of New Testament at new evangelical Trinity Evangelical Divinity School, Deerfield, Illinois. He is also a speaker at "The Gospel Coalition's" 2013 meeting. "The Gospel Coalition" is a hodge-podge of new evangelicals. Speakers at the Coalition's 2013 conference in Orlando, FL, include Shai Linne. Who is Shai Linne?

> *"Shai Linne is a recording artist with Lamp Mode Recordings, an independent Christian hip-hop record label whose mission is to highlight the character of God while* **presenting the gospel of Jesus Christ and a biblical worldview through hip-hop culture.** *Shai is a theologian, poet, and pastor-in-training, having recently completed a pastoral internship at* **Capitol Hill Baptist Church in Washington D.C.,** *where he is a member"*(emphasis added).[65]

REMEMBER, Capitol Hill Baptist is where Mark Dever is pastor! Calvary Baptist Seminary had Mark Dever as the keynote speaker in 2011 and in 2013 Calvary Seminary had D. A. Carson! Carson is a part of The Gospel Coalition where Shai Linne is a participant. Tim Jordan was a speaker at the 2010 GARBC conference! **All these streams meet in one muddy new evangelical river!** Also, at the 2013 conference in Orlando, Florida, we note:

> *"The Gospel Coalition gathering . . . are* **CCM's Keith Getty, charismatic C. J. Mahaney** *and* **Southern Baptist R. Albert**

---

[63]http://www.monergism.com/thethreshold/articles/bio/markdever.html

[64]http://www.advancingthechurch.org/speakers

[65]http://thegospelcoalition.org/2013/speakers#j_d_greear

Mohler Jr."[66]

Is this what the GARBC churches desire for their young people? One of Getty's songs is the Number 1 song among GARB churches in 2012.[67]

This is the trail that a weak and soft position of ecclesiastical separation will take! On this contemporary trail, walking TOGETHER HAND IN HAND ARE: the CCM singer/song writers, the Southern Baptists, the charismatics, and numerous other Baptist folk and denominations. The GARBC is a part of this. Jordan opened the door further for more new evangelical ecumenism into the churches which form the GARBC! Once this door is opened, it is almost impossible to shut!

A SOFT, WEAK position on ecclesiastical separation leads to a weak practice and this is the root of the PROBLEM OF WHICH CCM IS ONE OF ITS FRUITS. It seems CCM and its trappings has become an idol to which the churches within the CCM scene bow. All churches using CCM give the impression that they all follow a similar pattern. The leaders, singers, and most of the audience wear jeans (often with holes). Some wear beanies and definitely no ties. T-shirts seem to be a must. The girls do not wear dresses or skirts. There are lots of glaring lights. There are also screens with the words flashed on them, rather than using hymnals. There are raised hands, along with the rhythm and gyration of the musical beat. It is almost undistinguishable to know whether one is hearing a "Christian" song or one of the "world's" songs! And Spurgeon thought he had a downgrade!

> 1 John 2:15 *"Love not the world, neither the things that are in the world. If any man love the world, the love of the Father is not in him."*

CCM is of the world. If a church does not use CCM, it cannot win the youth, so say some. To get'em in, you must have the sound of music to which they are accustomed! This is nothing short of pragmatism!

God's Word says in Ephesians 5:5-11
"For this ye know, that no whoremonger, nor unclean person,

---

[66]Ibid.

[67]http://baptistbulletin.org/?p=24900

> nor covetous man, who is an idolater, hath any inheritance in the kingdom of Christ and of God. 6 Let no man deceive you with vain words: for because of these things cometh the wrath of God upon the children of disobedience. 7 Be not ye therefore partakers with them. 8 For ye were sometimes darkness, but now are ye light in the Lord: walk as children of light: 9 (For the fruit of the Spirit is in all goodness and righteousness and truth;) 10 Proving what is acceptable unto the Lord. 11 And **have no fellowship with** the unfruitful works of darkness, but rather **reprove** them."

1 Timothy 4:1 *"Now the Spirit speaketh expressly, that in the latter times some **shall depart from** the faith, giving heed to seducing spirits, and doctrines of devils."*

2 Timothy 2:19 *"Nevertheless the foundation of God standeth sure, having this seal, The Lord knoweth them that are his. And, Let every one that nameth the name of Christ **depart from** iniquity."*

CCM has certainly broken down the wall of ecclesiastical separation between the various Baptist groups and other denominations. In the Christen picket fence analogy, most of the pickets are now missing. The wall of Biblical ecclesiastical separation needs to be built again;

> *"So built we the wall; and all the wall was joined together unto the half thereof: for the people had a mind to work"* Nehemiah 4:6.

However, for this to occur, it will take new leadership with a heart's desire for holiness which demands a separation from the worldliness of CCM and all its trappings. Any leader seeking to rebuild this wall of Biblical separation **MUST** be aware that this will be an affront to the Sanballats of CCM ecumenism. There will be those who will mock and oppose just as those that Nehemiah endured. The use of CCM and the trappings that accompany it will lead to new evangelicalism, ecumenism, liberalism, and eventually apostasy. Some may dispute this statement, but time will prove it to be true.

Remember, God is not through with His faithful churches until the rapture, but until then:

> *"Be sober, **be vigilant**; because your adversary the devil, as a roaring lion, walketh about, seeking whom he may devour"*

(1Peter 5:8).

Remember, God also said, in 2 Corinthians 6:17,
"Wherefore come out from among them, and be ye separate, saith the Lord, and touch not the unclean thing; and I will receive you."

Whether it suits the culture or not, when a church strives to live a holy life before the Head of the church, **there will be a wall of ecclesiastical separation** between the Lord's church and the world.

Before closing, it is worth hearing the Prince of Preachers again when he said:

"I cannot suppose that at the last great day our Lord Jesus Christ will say to anyone, 'You were not worldly enough. You were too jealous over your conduct, and did not sufficiently conform to the world.' No, my brethren, such a wrong is impossible. He Who said, 'Be ye perfect, even as your Father which is in heaven is perfect,' has set before you a standard beyond which you can never go."

Index Of Key Words And Phrases

1 Corinthians 14:15. 24
1 Corinthians 14:7. 27
1 Corinthians 14:8. 26
1 Corinthians 15:52. 26
1 John 2:15. . . . . 29, 43, 47
1 Timothy 4:1. 48
144,000 persons, evangelists in Revelation. 3
15 different Literature Items of the GARBC. 40
1800's, when the Gnostic Critical Greek Text was developed. 44
1851, when Hort hated the Textus Receptus. 44
1972, the year Dr. Bennett had his music course from Mr. Bergerson. 3-5
1979, when Dr. and Mrs. Bennett began as Australian missionaries. iv, 39, 40
1983, the date Paul Tassell wrote a book. 40
1985, when Paul Tassell rejected Biblical separation. 41
1986 GARBC Conference, when Tassell rebuked churches for separation. 41
1987, the GARBC rejected its own 15 literature items as their position. . . 40
1995, a pastor approved Hill's statement. 14, 15, 38, 39
1Peter 5:8. 49
2 Timothy 2:19. 48
2009, first service in one CCM church. 12, 14, 30, 32, 34
2010 GARBC conference, Tim Jordan spoke. 14, 45, 46
2011, the GARBC began to back away from "Baptist". 37, 45, 46
2013, an article in an Australian paper. i, 7, 37, 46
6/25/90, Tassell stated his anti-separatist position. 41
8,000 differences between the Critical and Textus Receptus texts a book. . 44
A FEW NEW TESTAMENT SCRIPTURES CONCERNING MUSIC:. . . 24
a non-separatist, Richard Christen was, became GARBC National Rep. . . . 42
A Warning against CCM. . . . . ii, 1, 9, 31
Acknowledgments. . . . . ii, v
acoustic guitar, what CCM people use in their services. 22
Acts 16:25. . . . . 3, 4, 26
Acts 20:29-31. . . . . 1, 8
adoption of CCM, removed the Baptist name. 43
Advancing the Church Conference. 45
Agu Irukwu, a CCM follower. 35
Amillennial. 46
Anaheim, where the GARBC rejected their 15 literature items. 40

Andy Stanley is into CCM at his church. 12
Anne Marie Noyle, a BFTBC helper and proofreader from Canada. v
anti-separatist position of Paul Tassell and GARBC. 41
apostasy. 1, 32, 40, 41, 48
Apostle Paul. 1, 8
apostles' day. 4
APPRAISALS AND COMMENTS. 5
approved school of the GARBC, Dr. Bennett attended. 13
archaic. 38
armour of God. 2
assistant pastors should have proper view of music. 3
association, various. 13, 18, 39
Atlanta. 32
Australia. . . . . iii, iv, 39
Australia in 1979, Dr. Bennett became a missionary there. 39
Awana. 34
Baloche, Paul, CCM promoter. 14, 34
band, used in CCM churches. 18-22, 33
Baptist Bulletin, official organ of the GARBC. 13, 28, 31, 37
Baptist churches. 2, 11, 30, 39, 43
Baptist name, downplayed by GARBC now. 43
bass, used in CCM churches. 19, 22
BBF, Bible Baptist Fellowship. 18
BBFI, Bible Baptist Fellowship International. . . 11, 18-20, 30, 35, 37, 43, 44
be ye separate, a clear Bible command. 49
beanie, used in CCM churches. 34
beanies, used in CCM churches. 47
beat, strong, in CCM music. 29, 47
Beatles' Twist & Shout, a CCM song. 34
before 1970, most Baptist churches used the KJB. 43
Bennett, Dr. David, author of this book. . . . . 1, iii, iv, 44
Bergerson, Mr. Charles, Dr. Bennett's professor in music. 3-5
Best, Harold M., Wheaton College's music teacher. 6, 9
Bethlehem Baptist Church. 18
BFT #3084, *8000 Differences Between the CT and TR* by Dr. Moorman . . 44
BFT Phone: 856-854-4452. i
BIBLE FOR TODAY. . . . . i, iv, v
Bible For Today Baptist Church. . . . . i, iv, v
BIBLE FOR TODAY PRESS. i
Bible version changes when CCM comes in. 17, 42
Biblical separation, weakened in the present GARBC. 39-41, 48

Biblical worship should have proper music, not CCM................. 3
Bill Rudd, GARBC search committee chairman for National Rep........ 39
Bob Gray, Baptist pastor charged with pedophilia................... 20
break down the wall of separation, CCM does it.................... 9
BRENTON BROWN, CCM writer........................ 14, 32-34
broken down the wall of separation, CCM has done it.............. 48
Brown, Brenton, CCM writer............................. 14, 32-34
C. J. Mahaney, Charismatic CCM man. 46
Calvary Baptist Church in Lansdale, PA, where Tim Jordan is pastor..... 45
Calvary Baptist Seminary, in Lansdale, PA...................... 45, 46
Calvary Community Church, in CA where Brenton Brown attends.... 32, 33
Calvary Seminary, in Landsdale, PA........................... 46
Calvinists, weak separation. 43
Calvin's theology, weak separation and leaning toward CCM.......... 43
Candidate form that GARBC has prospective pastors fill out, compromise . 42
Capitol Hill Baptist Church, where Shai Linne is a member. 46
CARE, a CCM organization................................... 31, 35
CCM, Contemporary Christian Music..... 1-iv, 2, 7-9, 11-13, 16-24, 28-30,
                                        32-35, 37, 38, 42-44, 47, 48
CCM and the Churches. ii
CCM dangers... iv
CCM is of the world... 47
CCM is only a symptom....................................... 37
CCM is their death, of the churches that are using it. 22
CCM's Keith Getty. 46
cease criticizing, Tassell told the GARBC to, compromise groups. 41
Cedarville University, a compromising former GARBC school. 16, 41
Chandler, Matt, a Reformed Theology man......................... 42
change in the Bible version, with a change in music. 17
changed his position, Paul Tassell, on separation.................... 41
charismatic movement, many use CCM............... 29, 31, 43, 46, 47
charismatic C. J. Mahaney.................................... 46
charismatic gifts, many in CCM want these to increase............. 31, 43
charismatic movement uses CCM often........................... 29
Charles Bergerson (1918-2000) a music lecturer for Dr. Bennett. 3
Chicago Symphony, Bergerson was pianist there.................... 3
Chris Tomlin, a CCM composer. 14, 15, 32-34
CHRISTEN, Dr. Richard, GARBC's new National Representative. 39, 41, 48
Christian bands, used by CCM groups............................. 21
Christian hip-hop record label, used by CCM people. 46
Christianity Today, an article about Luther's music.................. 6

Christian's music appreciation, an important factor. 5
church groups, and their CCM music. 11
Church Life Worship Band. 20
church music, important choices. 2, 3, 5, 6, 29
Church music has changed to CCM. 3
Church music is changing to CCM. 29
CHURCH MUSIC TODAY, a section of the book. 6
Church Phone: 856-854-4747, Bible For Today Baptist Church. i
church youth music, moving to CCM. 5
Civic Auditorium, Harold Ockenga's first message on neo-evangelicalism. . 7
Clarke, Gary, a CCM man. 35
classical music. 4, 5
CLASSICAL MUSIC. 4, 5
Classical music was downgraded. 5
climate of worship, ever changing. 16
CLOSING THOUGHT, CCM is much the same in every place it is. 22
Collingswood, New Jersey, home of the Bible For Today Baptist Church. . . . i
Colossians 3:16. . . . . 24, 25
come out from among them, and be separate, a command of God. 49
Community Fellowship, a CCM group. 34
compromising evangelicals abound. 40
compromising speakers are invited by GARBC people. 41
Confluence, a place where all shades of belief come together. 31
Congregation, of Bible For Today Baptist Church. . . . . v, 6, 15, 18
Conservatory of Music, at Wheaton College, Best was director. 6
contemporary. . . . . iii, iv, 2, 6, 11, 15-18, 21,
                                                                                    42, 43, 47
Contemporary Christian Music. . . . . iii, iv
contemporary church music. 2
contemporary movement, gained momentum. 43
contemporary music. 16-18
corrupting, all false teaching. 9
Covenant Theology, Mark Dever's beliefs. 45
Credo-Baptist, Mark Dever is one. 45
Criswell, , W. A., Pastor First Baptist Church of Dallas. 11
Critical Greek text, developed in the 1800's by Westcott and Hort. 44, 46
criticize their compromises, GARBC is now departing from those who. . . . 41
cultural change, CCM part of this. 5
cultural fundamentalism, different from historic fundamentalism. 45
D. A. Carson, Calvary Seminary's 2013 keynote speaker. 46
D. A. Waite, Pastor of Bible For Today Baptist Church. . . . . i, iv

dance, used in CCM meetings. 35
Daniel, book of.. . . . . 14, 33
Dayton, Ohio, GARBC conference held there. 40
Dean Burgon Society, stands for the KJB and Hebrew and Greek under it. . iv
deceptive teachings and tactics, grievous wolves bring in. 8
Deerfield, Illinois, where new evangelical Trinity Divinity School is. 46
defeated for the Council, outspoken separatists were, from GARBC. 40
defended Cedarville College, Paul Tassell did. 41
degrading in its styling, CCM music is.. 5
departure of BBFI and GARBC from former positions. 44
Dever, Mark, a Southern Baptist and Calvinist. 45, 46
Devil.. . . . . 2, 6, 8, 48
Devil's WILES.. 2
differed on issues, but together on the gospel.. 43
different instruments used in CCM music. 22
disciples of these wolves, with unsound doctrine.. 9
distorting the truth. 9
diversity of theology, ecumenism.. 30
DIVORCED ITSELF FROM THE CHURCH, sound music did.. 4
do not seem to care who uses CCM, all diverse groups. 35
doctrinal differences, obliterated by CCM. 2
Doctrinal Statement of the GARBC is for separatism. 40
doctrinally divergent churches, bringing them together by CCM.. 2
Does It Matter?, Chapter IV of this book.. . . . . ii, 37
door is opened, of compromise, then impossible to shut. 47
downward course, of the GARBC. 39
Dr. David Bennett, missionary to Australia, and author of this book. iv
Dr. Lee Roberson, former pastor in Chattanooga, TN. 21
Dr. Mark Jackson, former interim GARBC National Representative.. 39
Dr. Paul Tassell, former GARBC National Representative, compromiser.. 39
Dr. Richard Christen, GARBC National Representative. 39, 41
Dr. Roberson, Lee, former pastor. 21
Dr. Tassell, Paul, compromise GARBC National Representative. 41
Dr. Warren Wiersbe, compromise speaker at GARBC meetings. 39
dress codes, none at CCM groups. 45
dressed down at CCM groups.. . . . . 21, 22, 33, 34
Driscoll, Mark, a Reformed Theology man. 42
dropped the name "Baptist".. . . . . 17, 37
dropping of the name Baptist. 37
drums, used at CCM meetings. 15, 19, 21, 22, 28
ecclesiastical separation dropped by CCM people. 9, 39, 41-44, 47-

49

ecclesiastical separatism, the wall is broken down. 38
ecumenism brought on by CCM. 2, 15, 17, 29-33, 47, 48
ecumenism through music of CCM. 2
ecumenist, Tim Hughes. 35
Egypt, a picture of the world. 29, 34, 44
electric guitar, used at CCM meetings.. . . . . 19, 22
electric key boards, used at CCM meetings. 22
English Bible but also the Hebrew and Greek underlying it are affected. . . 44
English Standard Version, a perverted version used by many.. 17
entertainment, given by CCM emphasis. 6, 18, 22
Ephesian elders, Paul warned them of those within and without.. . . . . . . 1, 8
Ephesians 5:19. . . . . 2, 6, 24, 25
Ephesians 5:5-11. 47
Ephesians 6:11. 2
Ephesus. 1, 8, 9
ESV, English Standard Version, from corrupt Greek Text. 17, 38
Evangelicals, a repudiation of separatism. 7, 40, 46
evangelists. 8
Executive Committee members of the Dean Burgon Society. iv
expedient fundamentalists don't want to fight for the faith. 40
expert musician, Dr. Bennett is not. . . . . iii, 3
e-mail: BFT@BibleForToday.org our e-mail address.. i
Fair Oaks Baptist Church. 18
fax: 856-854-2464, our Bible For Today FAX number. i
February, 2013, the GARBC council diminished "Baptist" in name. . . . 7, 37
Fellowship Connection, Willow Creek Association. 18
fence, a picket, rather than a wall of separation. 39, 43, 48
finding a pastor, for GARBC, compromise questions asked. 42
First Baptist Church of Dallas, W. E. Criswell former pastor. 11
footnotes, of this book will help further research. . . . . iii, 29
Foreword of this book, by Pastor D. A. Waite. . . . . ii, iv, 7
formerly fundamental and separatist, churches before CCM took over. iv
from outside, enemies would come in. 8
from WITHIN, enemies would come in. 1, 2, 8, 9, 29
from WITHOUT, enemies would come in. 1, 2, 8, 9, 29
FRUITS, one of is no separation when CCM comes in.. 47
fundamental, churches were before CCM came in. iv
fundamentalism, Ockenga affirmed, but went to new evangelicalism. 7, 39, 45
GARB, group of former separatist churches. 11, 13, 15, 17, 20, 28, 30, 31, 35,
37-47

GARBC, formerly a separatist group......... 11, 13, 15, 17, 20, 28, 30, 31, 35, 37-47
GARBC is not a closed club, GARBC's John Greening said........... 45
GARBC's 1987 Annual Meeting in Anaheim, rejected their 15 items..... 40
GARBC's change, no longer warned against new evangelicalism........ 41
Gary Clarke, a CCM performer.................................. 35
gays, some outspoken on.. 12
George Beverly Shea, singer for Billy Graham, Bergerson sang with...... 3
George Truett, former pastor in First Baptist Church in Dallas......... 11
GEORGIA (SBC), church where Andy Stanley pastors................ 12
Getty, Keith, CCM song writer....................... 14, 29, 30, 46
Giglio, Louie, CCM song writer........................... 14, 30, 32
girls do not wear dresses or skirts in CCM groups................... 47
give forth a warning, the purpose of this book...................... 9
glaring lights, used with CCM groups............................ 47
Gnostic Critical Greek New Testament Text, used in modern Bibles. 44
good music, going out of popularity.............................. 4
Gospel Coalition, Reformed Theology group. 42, 46
Grace Theological Seminary, Winona Lake, Indiana.................. 3
Grand Rapids, Michigan, GARBC conference where Tassell changed. ... 41
Gray, Bog, charged with pedophilia.............................. 20
Great Shepherd, the Lord Jesus Christ............................ 8
Greek text underlying the KJB vs. the new versions. 44, 46
Greek text underlying the King James............................ 44
Greening, John, GARBC National representative................. 42, 45
guitars, used in CCM groups. 20-22, 28
Gumbel, Nicky, CCM writer. 35
gyrations, used at CCM meetings............................ 28, 29
hand held microphones, used at CCM meetings.................... 20
HAND IN HAND, compromising doctrines. 47
Harold M. Best, music director at Wheaton College. 6
HARP, as used in the Bible. 27
HARPS, as used in the Bible. 27, 28
have no fellowship with unfruitful works of darkness. 48
Hebrews 12:19.. 26
Hebrews 2:12... 25
Highlands worship team, using CCM............................ 22
Hill, Roland, GARBC related Reformed Theology believer. 38, 46
Hillsong, CCM group.. 35
hip-hop, used in CCM groups. 46
hip-hop culture, of CCM. 46

historic fundamentalism, versus cultural fundamentalism. 45
hoary head, a crown of glory. 23
hodge-podge, truth and error mixed together. 46
holiness demands separation from the world.. 48
holy life demands separation form the world, not CCM. 49
Hort, teamed with Westcott to form an erroneous Greek Text. 44
Houston, Joel, a CCM man. 35
How far will CCM take the churches? all the way to apostasy. 35
Huffman was correct about removal the pickets in the fence of separation.. 39
Hughes, Tim, a CCM writer. 14, 30, 34, 35
humanism, CCM can lead to it. 5
hymnals, not used by CCM churches. 47
hymning God, the New Testament writers urged this. 3
hymn-tunes, arrangements from classical music. 4
hypocritical worship, is CCM. 6
I ceased not to warn the elders of Ephesus day by day said Paul. 1, 8
incompetent musicians, we have many who turn to CCM.. 6
independent Baptist.. . . . . 11, 20, 21, 30, 43
independent Baptist church. 21
INDEPENDENT BAPTIST: TRINITY BAPTIST, JACKSONVILLE,
    FLORIDA. 20
Index of Words and Phrases, a most important part of this book. ii
instrumental music, used in CCM groups. 23
Internet attender, Anne Marie Noyle and others. . . . . v, 2, 11, 40
Internet attender, Anne Marie Noyle and others. v
Introduction to Music, by Mr. Bergerson of Dr. Bennett. 3
invited compromising speakers, Cedarville College has done. 41
irresponsible fundamentalists who invite compromisers to their group 40
Irukwu, Agu, a CCM man. 35
it does matter, the type of music used. 2
Jackson, Dr. Mark, of GARBC. 39
James 1:17.. 4
James 5:13.. 25
jeans, used in CCM groups 47
jeans (often with holes), used in CCM groups. 47
Jerusalem church, in the. 8
Jesus House, a CCM group 35
Joel Houston, a CCM man. 35
John Greening, GARBC National Representative.. . . . . 42, 45
John Piper, a Reformed Theology leader. 42
Jordan, Jim, a CCM man. 15, 45-47

jump the ship, of ecclesiastical separation. 42
Keith Getty, a CCM writer. 14, 30, 46
Keller, Tim, a CCM writer. 42
keyboards, used in CCM music. 22
King James Bible, the most accurate of all English versions. . . . . i, 38, 43, 44
Lamp Mode Recordings, CCM recording group 46
Lansdale, PA, where Calvary Baptist Seminary resides. 45
large screen, part of CCM groups. 19
leather jacket, used in CCM groups. 34
liberalism, each church is one pastor away from it. 1, 22, 40, 48
Lindale, Texas, a place where CCM group is found. 34
Linne, Shai, a CCM man. 46
Literature Items of GARBC, renounce by them as to their beliefs. 40
local church, one pastor away from apostasy. 1, 2, 8, 28, 45
lots of lights used in CCM churches. 34
LOUD music in CCM. 13, 19, 21, 22, 27
LOUD ON PURPOSE BAND! in CCM music. 19
loud sounds, in CCM music. 13
LOUDNESS. in CCM music. 29, 34
Louie Giglio, CCM writer. 14, 30, 32
Louie and Shelley Giglio, CCM writers. 32
LOUIS GIGLIO, CCM writer. 32
low the wall, see how low the wall of separation can be made. 43
lowered, separation wall lowered by CCM. 38
Luke 15:25. 24
LUTHER'S MUSIC, a heading for discussion. 6
Luther's total position given on music. 6
Mahaney, C. J., a charismatic CCM man. 46
Mandate, a CCM group. 31
Mark 14:26. 26
Mark Dever, a Southern Baptist speaker at GARBC. 45, 46
Mark Driscoll, a Reformed Theology man. 42
Mark Jackson, interim GARBC National Representative. 39
masters degree, Bergerson earned it at Grace Seminary. 3
Matt Chandler, a Reformed Theology man. 42
MATT REDMAN, CCM song writer. 14, 32, 34
Matthew 24:31. 26
Matthew 6:2. 26
mega churches, most are into CCM. 12
mega-church, Memorial church is not. 15
Methodist, use same CCM as other churches. 2, 11

microphones, many in CCM groups. 20, 22
militant, GARBC used to be. 39
minor mode, tunes from apostles day sung in this mode 4
misuse of history in interpreting Luther's music. 6
mixed multitude, of CCM people. 30, 31, 34
Mohler, R. Albert, a CCM man.. 47
Moody Bible Institute. 3, 41
Mount of Olives. 26, 28
muddy new evangelical river, GARBC has now into. 46
multimedia experiences, used in CCM. 18
MUSIC in Scripture and CCM. . . . . ii-iv, 2-9, 11-13, 15-18, 21, 23,
                                                     24, 26, 28-35, 45, 47
music in contemporary idioms, like CCM.. 6
MUSIC is ONE wile, method, or trick of the Devil. 2
music is the precursor to apostasy, as in CCM music. 32
music of churches today, does not fit Biblical pattern.. 28
music teachers, should have proper music understanding. 3
music used in various churches is the same CCM. 2, 3
musicians of CCM.. . . . . ii, 6, 15, 23, 28, 29, 31, 32, 35
MUSICK, verses used in the Bible. 24
name Baptist, removed by GARBC if desired.. . . . . 17, 37, 43
NASV, New American Standard Version. 38
National Representative, of the GARBC.. 39-41
Nehemiah. 39, 48
Nehemiah 4:6. 48
neither sacred nor popular, classical music. 4
new evangelicalism, departure from Biblical separatism. 22, 48
new evangelicals, depart from Biblical separatism. 46
New Frontiers, a CCM group. 31
New Horizon festival, a CCM group.. 31
new styles of music, including CCM.. 5
New Testament Church 9
new versions. 38, 44
new-Calvinists, weak on separation. 43
new-evangelicalism, every church is one pastor away from it.. . . . . 1, 8
Niagara Falls Conference GARBC conference, Tassell changed position. . 41
Nicky Gumbel, charismatic CCM man. 35
night of worship, CCM style. 35
no longer wanted to practice separation, Tassell told GARBC in 1990. . . . 41
no longer warned against neo-evangelicalism, Tassell in 1990. 41
no ties, uniform of the CCM people. 47

noise, lots of it at CCM meetings......................... 15, 28, 33, 34

non-denominational, Community Fellowship........................ 18

notation by which music is preserved............................... 4

notes taken by Dr. Bennett from Mr. Bergerson..................... 3, 4

November 2011, GARBC removes need for "Baptist" in title.......... 37

Noyle, Anne Marie, proofreader. v

Numbers 11:5.. 29

obedient fundamentalists, we should all be. 40

Ockenga, Harold John, founder of neo-evangelicalism compromise..... 7, 8

October 15, 2012, date of many CCM songs used by GARBC churches.14, 28

October, 2012, issue of GARBC's *Baptist Bulletin*.................. 31

of your own selves shall men arise, Acts 20:29-31................... 1, 8

official organ of GARBC, *Baptist Bulletin*. 13

one pastor away from liberalism, any church is...................... 1

ONE STEP AWAY, a section heading. 1

opened the door for more compromise............................ 47

Orders: 1-800-John 10:9, for the Bible For Today materials............ i

organ music, addressed by Tim Jordan. 45

Orlando, FL, place of compromise conference. 46

ought not to be used or allowed by the Christian, CCM music. 5

outspoken separatists of GARBC were defeated for the Council of 18. ... 40

Pasadena, CA, where Ockenga founded new evangelicalism in 1948. 7

PASSION CITY CHURCH, a CCM church in Atlanta. 32

Pastor D. A. Waite, of the 𝔅ible 𝔉or 𝔗oday 𝔅aptist 𝔆hurch............ i, iv

Pathways to Power, Tassell's 1983 book.......................... 40

Paul and Silas in the prison, music probably used by them in prison....... 4

PAUL BALOCHE, CCM writer. 14, 34

Paul Tassell, former GARBC National Representative compromiser. . 39, 42

Pentecostal, raising of hands no longer makes you one, CCM does same. . 34

perverse things, men shall arise from within to speak. 1, 8, 37

perverted doctrines, taught by people from within.................... 9

Peter Wilson, Pentecostal CCM man............................. 35

picket fence of separation rather than a wall. 39, 48

pickets are missing from the fence of separation. 43

pickets are now missing from fence of separation. 48

Piper, John, Reformed Theology leader............................ 42

popularization of religion, brought on by CCM...................... 5

power of music is undeniable.................................... 21

pragmatism, getting people in by any means, including CCM.......... 47

praise team, used in CCM meetings............................ 15, 19

preachers, should be taught sound music.................... 3, 8, 23, 49

precursor to apostasy, unity of theology and music, is a 32
Preface to this book . . . . ii, iii
Presbyterian churches, music is the same as in other groups 2, 11
Presbyterian churches, music is the same as in other groups 2
Prince of Preachers, Spurgeon. 49
private meeting, in 1990 where Tassell told he changed separation stance . . 41
problem, CCM is not, only a symptom. 1, 2, 29, 37, 44, 47
professions of faith, numerous, but removing "Baptist" 43
Proverbs 16:31 23
Publisher's Data, for this book. ii
R. Albert Mohler Jr., Souther Baptist CCM man. 47
raised hands, used in CCM meetings 13, 20, 22, 47
raising of the hands, used in CCM meetings as well as elsewhere. 34
rapture, God is not through with faithful churches until the. 48
rebuke GARBC churches, Tassell did, for too much separation 41
Received Greek New Testament Text that underlies our KJB. 44
recording artist, Shai Linne 46
Redman, Beth, CCM writer 14, 32, 34
reformed theology people also into CCM 31, 38, 42
Reformed men, also into CCM. 42
Reformed theology, those believing it also into CCM. 38, 42
relinquished the name Baptist when into CCM, some have. 43
reprove them, the unfruitful works of darkness (Ephesians 5:11) 48
repudiated almost everything, Baptist who go into CCM. 43
repudiation of separatism, Ockenga's, in 1948 meeting. 7
Revelation 1:10 27
Revelation 14:2 27
Revelation 14:3 . . . . 3, 25
Revelation 15:2 28
Revelation 15:3 25
Revelation 4:1 27
Revelation 5:8 27
Revelation 5:9 25
Revelation 8:13 27
Revelation 9:14 27
rhythm and beat of CCM are of the world 29, 47
Richard Christen, former GARBC National Representative 39, 41
Roberson, Lee, former Tennessee pastor. 21
rock and folk styling should be shunned 5
Roland Hill, early Christian warned about separation walls lowered. 38
Romans 15:9 . . . . 3, 24

Rudd, Bill, GARBC search committee chairman...................... 39
SACRED MUSIC, a unit heading, from Mr. Bergerson. 3
Saddleback, a kind of "worship". 34
Saddleback worship and music conference in 2009.................. 34
Sanballats of CCM ecumenism. 48
SANG, as used in the KJB...................................... 3, 26
Saylorville Church, its use of CCM.............................. 17
SBC, Southern Baptist Convention. 11, 12, 20, 21, 35, 37, 43
SBC, FIRST BAPTIST, DALLAS TX, church using CCM now......... 11
school teachers, should know sound music. 3
screen, big, used in CCM meetings. 13, 15, 19
screens, big, used in CCM meetings................... 12, 20, 22, 33, 47
Scriptural separation from apostasy, used to be taught by Tassell....... 40
scruffy look, of those at CCM meetings........................... 33
Search Committee Chairman for GARBC National Rep, Bill Rudd. 39
secondary separation, Tassell formerly stood for it. 39, 40
sending church for Dr. Bennett was Paul Tassell's former church........ 39
sentimental songs, not necessarily Scriptural....................... 6
separation and music, a moving away for years now. 13
separation from disobedient brethren, Tassell no longer believe this...... 41
separatist, we should be, but many are no longer....... iv, 32, 34, 39-42, 45
Set goals on the conservative side. 6
Shai Linne, a CCM man... 46
Shea, George Beverly, Bergerson sang in a quartet with him at Moody. ... 3
SHEEP, Christians as................................. 8, 15, 29, 30
sick congregational singing, in some churches........................ 6
SING, as used in the KJB...................... 3, 15, 22, 24, 25, 29
singing, in CCM churches. 2, 6, 7, 15, 21, 24-26, 28, 34
singing and making melody, Scripturally called for........... 2, 7, 24, 25
skilled musician and a composer, Harold Best was. 6
slippery slope, CCM is to further ecumenism. 17, 22
social involvement, Ockenga called for in 1948...................... 7
sociological, political, and economic areas, Ockenga called for in 1948.... 7
soft and weak on ecclesiastical separation......................... 43
soft position of ecclesiastical separation, the GARBC................. 47
song, used in CCM groups........................ 3, 6, 7, 15, 25, 47
songs, used in CCM groups........... 2, 3, 5-7, 13, 20-22, 24-26, 28, 29, 34, 47
songs of Zion, we must choose these............................. 7
Soul Survivor Church, a CCM church............................ 35
Southern Baptist, using CCM and little separation.............. 11, 45, 46

Southern Baptist R. Albert Mohler Jr, into CCM. 47
speak on your platform, who you invite is important. 40
spiritual songs, mentioned in Scripture. 2, 3, 7, 24-26
Spring Harvest, CCM group. 31
Spurgeon, Charles Haddon quoted. 7, 23, 28, 47
Stanley, Andy, uses CCM in his church. 12
streams meet, in one huge compromise. 46
strict and harsh, separation of earlier days is too. 38
STUART TOWNSEND, CCM writer. 14, 31
SUNG, as found in the KJB. 3, 4, 25, 26
surgeon's sterilization of hands and instruments before surgery. 41
Sword of the Lord, printed Bob Gray's sermons. 20
Sydney Daily Telegraph, article about teen music. 7
symptom, CCM is, not the problem. 1, 37
Table of Contents for this book. ii
Tassell, Paul, GARBC's National Representative who went soft. 39-42
teachers should have a sound view of music. 3, 8
TEEN'S IPOD, can tell you if they're in trouble. 7
Textus Receptus, the Greek text underlying the KJB. 44
THE BATTLE FOR THE BIBLE, by Harold Lindsell. 7
The Highlands, a CCM church. 21, 22
The Musicians of CCM And Where They Lead, a chapter title. ii
THE SEVEN, a unit heading. 30, 32
theological liberalism and compromising accommodation. 40
this kind of music, CCM, should not be used by anyone. 5
Thousand Oaks, CA, a CCM there is typical of them. 32
three areas that are relinquished by adopting CCM. 43
Tim Hughes, CCM writer. 14, 34, 35
Tim Jordan, pastor in Landsdale, PA, spoke at GARBC 2010 . . . . 45, 46
Tim Keller, Reformed Theology man. 42
tired of 'scrubbing for surgery' Paul Tassell was, no separation. 41
TODAY'S SECULAR MUSIC?, a unit heading. 7
Together for the Gospel, a Reformed Theology group. 42
Tomlin, Chris, a CCM writer. 14, 15, 32-34
too much separation, Tassell rebuked GARBC churches for it. 41
too strict and harsh, Bible separation is said to be. 38
Townsend, Stuart, CCM writer. 14, 31
traditional music blended with CCM. 15, 16, 21, 42
transforms their church for the worse, CCM does. iv
trappings of CCM. 43, 47, 48
trends in music, part of a cultural change. 5

trial for pedophilia, Bob Gray was about to have a. 20

Tribe of Judah, a CCM group. 35

Trinity Evangelical Divinity School, in Deerfield, Illinois. 46

Truett, George, former pastor of First Baptist Church in Dallas. 11

TRUMPET, as used in the KJB. 26, 27

turning away, meaning of "perverse". 9

two-foot thick wall, of separation should be for the GARBC. 39

TYPE OF MUSIC PLAYED, an important part of evaluation. 2

T-shirt, worn by CCM groups. 34

T-shirts, worn by CCM groups. 47

unity of theology, often leads to apostasy. 32

unpopular, a person questioning music. 6

used to attract people toward Christ, some thought CCM could be. 5

various denominations getting together, through CCM. 9

very conservative in his music, Mr. Bergerson. 3

vile Textus Receptus leaning, Hort had when only a young man. 44

villainous Textus Receptus, Hort called it when a young man. 44

volume of CCM is loud. 2

W. A. Criswell, former pastor of First Baptist Church of Dallas, SBC. . . . 11

Waite, Pastor D. A., Mrs. Waite, and D. A. Waite, Jr. . . . . i, iv, v

wall of ecclesiastical separation. 9, 39, 43, 48, 49

walls of separation, Roland Hill did not want these to be broken down. . . . 38

warn every one night and day, Paul did to the Ephesians. 1, 8

WARNING FOR TODAY?, a unit heading. 9

Website: www.BibleForToday.org for our Bible For Today ministry. i

websites listed in the footnotes for more material. 29

Westcott and Hort, founders in 1881, of the Gnostic Critical Greek Text. . 44

WHAT IS THE GOAL OF CCM?, a unit heading. 7

what, where, how, and why of music, Mr. Bergerson's questions. 4

Wheaton College, Harold Best taught music there. 6

WHERE WILL THIS ALL END?, once you begin with CCM. 35

Wiersbe, Warren, spoke at GARBC conference. 39

WILES (methods) of the Devil. 2

will not follow in practice, GARBC regarding separation. 40

Willow Creek Association, a CCM group. 18

Wilson, Peter, a CCM man. 35

win the youth, CCM cannot. 47

Winona Lake, Indiana, where Mr. Bergerson got his master's degree. 3

WITHIN, forces, to do damage. 1, 2, 7-9, 13, 29, 37, 47

WITHOUT, forces to do damage. 1, 2, 5, 8, 9, 23, 27, 29, 37

wolf sees the sheep, to gratify his pleasure. 8

wolves enter into the flock to harm........................ 1, 8, 9, 37

Word of Life, not to be criticized by Tassell........................ 41

world is influencing the church rather than church influencing the world.... 6

WORLDLY MUSICAL VOICES, must be discerned. 5

worship, CCM style.................. 3, 5, 6, 11, 13, 16, 18-20, 22, 23, 28, 31, 33-35, 42

worship band used in CCM groups........................... 18-20

worship degree program, taught at Cedarville University, Cedarville, OH.. 16

worship experience, of CCM style. 22

worship leader, used by CCM groups........................... 16

Worship Together, a CCM group........................... 33, 35

youth, influenced by CCM. 5, 47

youth music, influenced by CCM. 5

Yvonne Sanborn Waite, wife of Pastor D. A. Waite.................. v

Dr. David C. Bennett

- **The Need**. This little booklet points out the growing acceptance of Contemporary Christian Music (CCM) in churches that were formerly fundamental and separatist. This CCM has brought with it the lowering of standards in these churches that have begun to use it. Dr. Bennett has given many facts to enable the readers to try to keep CCM completely out of their churches.

- **The Author.** Dr. David Bennett is the author of this book. He has been one of the missionaries of the 𝔅𝔦𝔟𝔩𝔢 𝔣𝔬𝔯 𝔗𝔬𝔡𝔞𝔶 𝔅𝔞𝔭𝔱𝔦𝔰𝔱 𝔠𝔥𝔲𝔯𝔠𝔥 for many years. Our church is his "sending church." Since 1979, he and his wife, Pam, have been faithfully serving the Lord Jesus Christ in the land of Australia. He has two churches and a radio ministry there. He is also one of our faithful Executive Committee members of the Dean Burgon Society (DBS).

- **The Book's Format.** I have taken Dr. Bennett's book and put it into a format that could be used for the printing of the book. Though this has taken some time and patience, it was necessary to be done before it could be sent to the publishers.

- **The Book's Usefulness.** It is our hope and prayer that this book might be used of the Lord to convince and encourage even further those who are concerned about music in their churches. It will equip the reader with important facts to enable them to warn others of the CCM dangers before this music completely transforms their church for the worse.

- **The Readers.** It is hoped that those who receive and read this book might encourage many others to get the book, read it, and urge others to read it as well.